Dictionary of the
Occult

GEDDES & GROSSET

This edition published 1999 by Geddes & Grosset
Reprinted 2002

© 1996 Geddes and Grosset,
David Dale House, New Lanark ML11 9DJ, Scotland

Cover image of Fire by Frederic Didillon,
courtesy of the Telegraph Colour Library

ISBN 1 85534 279 0

Printed and bound in the UK

Introduction

Knowledge is power. 'I know something you don't know' is a well-known childish chant, but it is mirrored in the adult world by the respect, and sometimes fear, claimed by and given to those who have special knowledge. To acquire knowledge is not necessarily easy. Some forms require the memorising of huge amounts of facts, and others demand complex thought-patterns. But whether it is easy or not, worth knowing or not, there is no doubt at all that, throughout history, those who know (always a small minority) have been concerned to keep their knowledge private from those (always the great majority) who do not have it.

The lore of the occult is no different in this from any other area of knowledge, and in fact is one of the least open. This can be seen in the word 'hermetic', so often encountered in writings on the occult. 'Hermetic' means 'belonging to Hermes' – Hermes Trismegistus was the legendary founder of alchemy – but has come to refer specifically to the hermetic seal, in which the alchemist heated the neck of his glass vessel until it was soft, then twisted it carefully until it formed a completely airtight seal on the contents. As with the contents of the flask, so with the elements of knowledge. They were carefully guarded and the would-be learner had to be first accepted then pass through a lengthy apprenticeship. It was not a simple and straightforward path. The adept's understanding and acumen was often being tested. Much of what we see as 'mumbo-jumbo' in occult lore may be deliberate, in order to conceal from too-eager intelligences what was regarded as highly secret and perhaps dangerous information. In the same way, the builders of the pyramids used to construct false doors and decoy passages to lure tomb-robbers away from the chambers where treasures lay under the protection of the gods.

The dictionary definition of occult is 'kept secret; beyond the range of ordinary knowledge; involving the supernatural, mystical or magical'. Occult knowledge today is based on the residue left from the growth and spread of science and religion during the past three thousand years. Until the development of the ancient Greek civilisation, all science was a form of magic. People knew in a practical way that certain things worked – they could pound grains in a mortar to make flour; they could make bows and arrows. But what made the crops grow? Why did the arrow sometimes hit its target and sometimes not? How could one ensure that next time it would do better? Every age of civilisation has provided its own best answers to such questions. Wise men have brooded on them, passed on their knowledge to sons or disciples, in time forming priesthoods. For centuries the Maya priests of Central America were able to predict the eclipses of Sun and Moon, after long observation and deduction. But they allowed the populace to believe that the Moon was being eaten by a magic jaguar, and that only the rites of the priests could prevent it from being devoured forever. Needless to say, the respect, the income and the power of the priesthood were all enhanced as a result. This is not to say that the priests were cynical exploiters of the people's ignorance. They put enormous thought and effort into their calendar and used it as a basis of prediction for such vital matters as the coming of rain and the success of the maize harvest.

In most societies, as time passed, areas of knowledge were removed from the secret zone to become public property. Exploration of the earth, discovery of the cosmos, the revelations of religion in the Bible and the Koran, all tended to reduce the stock of occult lore. But they did not eliminate it. Even in religion, the urge to explore and refine led to much creative and speculative thought, as with the GNOSTICS, which was frowned on, forbidden and persecuted by the religious authorities. The occult tradition has evolved with other fields of knowledge, and NEW AGE thinking has given it a new dimension. The urge towards the practicable and the provable, which has characterised the rise of modern technology and science, has inevitably led to a counter-reaction towards the mystical, the Earth-related and the natural. Ironically, it is the achievements of modern technology that have made possible the fusion of different – though often similar – traditions and teachings from all over the world that characterise occult study today. The word for this, in religion, is SYNCRETISM, and it applies with equal force to the occult. This immense variety of traditional teachings, with more being brought in all the time, makes the present era one of great interest and potential for students of the occult. Will the combination of all these millennia-old ways of thought, ways of seeing the universe, lead to a new and definitive synthesis? Time will tell. It seems that, for the human race, there will always be a search for the truth beyond the truth, for the secret pattern that must lie behind even the latest and most revolutionary discovery.

A

ABADDON
The name of the demon identified as the 'angel' of the bottomless pit in the Bible, Revelation 9:11.

ABIGOR
The name of a demon, conjured for his power to foretell the future and to provide military aid and advice.

ABRACADABRA
A Kabbalistic charm (*see* KABBALAH), possibly derived from the initials of the Hebraic words *Ab*, *Ben* and *ruach a Cadesch* ('Father, Son and Holy Ghost').

ABRAXAS
A mystical word, possibly of GNOSTIC origins, which expresses gematrically (*see* GEMATRIA) the number 365 and is linked with the solar cycle. The word is associated with the image of a man with the head of a cock holding a shield and whip. The image is often found on gems or stones for use in AMULETS.

ADAMASTOR
The name of the spirit of the storm-lashed Cape of Good Hope, which prophesies doom for those seeking to voyage beyond the Cape to India.

ADEPT
A person who is 'skilled' in occult wisdom. In alchemical lore there are always eleven adepts. *See* MAHATMA.

ADJURATION
A formula used in conjuring or exorcising evil spirits, by which the demon is commanded, in the name of the Christian God, to do or say what the magician or exorcist demands.

ADYTUM
In Greek this term denotes the holiest part of a temple and is used in occultism to refer to the holiest area of an initiation centre.

AEROMANCY
The art of foretelling future events by the observation of atmospheric phenomena, such as wind currents and cloud formation. *See* AUSTROMANCY.

AETITES
A magical stone, supposedly found in the neck or stomach of an eagle, that was thought to offer protection in childbirth.

AFRIT
In Islamic lore, the second most powerful class of devil-DJINS, of gigantic size and malevolent natures. They are derived from ancient Egyptian spirits of desert sandstorms.

AGATE
This quartz gemstone, possibly named after the river in Sicily where it is found, is said to have the power to turn the possessor invisible, and to offer protection in battle. The stone was consequently widely used in the art of TALISMANS.

AGATHODEMON
A good spirit worshiped by the Egyptians under the shape of a serpent with a human head.

AGE OF AQUARIUS
The supposed two-thousand-year period of enlightenment, peace and love heralded by the entry of the Sun into the zodiacal sign of Aquarius. Astrologers disagree on the date of the start of period – dates range from 1904 to 2160. The term was popular during the 1960s, a decade marked by social and political upheaval and increased interest in spiritual exploration and alternative lifestyles. *See also* NEW AGE.

AGRIPPA, CORNELIUS (1486–1535)
An occultist of the sixteenth century, born in Cologne, Germany. He was a profound student of the KABBALAH, and was particularly obsessed by the science of GEMATRIA. He became a doctor of divinity, but was suspected of heresy and fled from Germany to England. By the age of twenty-four, he had written his great treatise *On Occult Philosophy*, although it was not published for another twenty years. As with other great doctors of the occult, many wild stories grew up about Agrippa's magic powers. He was said to have been visited by the WANDERING JEW in his eternal roaming. Agrippa appears to have considered himself as a seer and diviner, and one of

his divining methods was to identify criminals by means of a device like a sieve, which, when suspended, turned towards those of a criminal character.

AHRIMAN
The demon of lies in Zoroastrian lore (*see* ZOROASTER), locked in eternal struggle with AHURA MAZDA. He is linked to the dragon or serpent form of SATAN, conquered by Saint Michael.

AHURA MAZDA
In the Zoroastrian scheme of things (*see* ZOROASTER), the source of creation and of good, who is also known as Ormuzd.

AKASHA
In Hinduism and Buddhism, the all-pervasive life principle or space of the universe. Hindu philosophy interprets the Akasha as the ether, the fifth and subtlest element which permeates the universe. In Buddhism the Akasha is space, both space bounded by the material world and a form of space that is unlimited and indefinable, which contains the material world. The concept was introduced to the West in the early twentieth century by Helena P. BLAVATSKY, cofounder of the Theosophical Society (*see* THEOSOPHY), who likened the Akasha to other interpretations of the universal life force by occultists through the ages, such as the QUINTESSENCE, that luminous fifth element (invisible to ordinary sight) which was seen as binding together in union or pact the other four elements. According to Blavatsky, the Akasha forms the ANIMA MUNDI and constitutes the soul and animal spirit of mankind.

An important related term is the so-called Akashic Chronicles (sometimes the Akashic Records) which, according to theosophy, are the historical records of all world events and personal experiences of all thoughts and deeds that have taken place on the earth. These are indelibly imprinted upon the Akasha and may under normal circumstances be read only by ADEPTS or initiates. Rudolf STEINER, for example, claimed to have accessed the Akashic Records for his descriptions of the mythical lost civilisations of ATLANTIS and LEMURIA.

ALASTOR
In ancient Roman demonology this is the name given to the evil GENIUS of a house. In the ancient Greek period the word meant 'avenging god'.

ALBERICH
The name of the king of the dwarves in Scandinavian mythology, popularised as the thief of the magic ring of gold in the *Niebelungenlied* operatic saga by the German composer Richard Wagner (1813–83).

ALBERTUS MAGNUS (*c*.1200–1280)
Legend would have him a magician, but in fact this famous German scholar, known from the breadth of his knowledge as the *Doctor Universalis*, did not stray from the path of religious correctness, and was canonised during the twentieth century. His great achievement was to link the philosophical tradition of Aristotle with the principles of Catholic theology.

ALCHEMY
An ancient pseudoscience concerned with the transmutation of base metals into gold and with the discovery of both a single cure for all diseases and a way to prolong life indefinitely. Symbolically, alchemy is a mystical art for human spiritual transformation into a higher form of being. Alchemy emerged

in China and in Egypt during the early centuries of this era. In China it was associated with Taoist philosophy and purported to transmute base metals into gold by use of a 'medicine'. The gold so produced was thought to have the ability to cure diseases and to prolong life. In Egypt, the methods of transmutation of metals were kept secret by temple priests. Those recipes became widely known (second century) at the academy in Alexandria. Alchemy had its basis in the skills of Egyptian artisans, Eastern mysticism and Aristotelian theory of composition of matter. Aristotle taught that all matter was composed of four elements: water, earth, fire and air. According to his theory, different materials found in nature had different ratios of these four elements. Therefore, by proper treatment a base metal could be changed into gold. These ideas were further supported by astrological speculations from Mesopotamia. Astrologers believed that celestial bodies – the Sun, the Moon and the stars – had a profound influence on the activities of humans. Thus, for alchemists to transmute metals effectively, the heavenly bodies had to be in a favourable configuration.

In the eighth and ninth centuries Chinese, Greek and Alexandrine alchemical lore entered the Arab world. The Arab alchemists modified the Aristotelian concept of four elements by postulating that all metals were composed of two immediate components: sulphur and mercury. They also adopted the Chinese alchemists' concept of a PHILOSOPHER'S STONE – a medicine that could turn a 'sick' (base) metal into gold and also act as an elixir of life. Arab alchemical treatises, such as those by the Persian physicians al-Razi (886–925) and Avicenna (980–1036) were popular during the Middle Ages.

With the fall of Rome, Greek science and philosophy declined in western Europe. However, close contact with Arabs in Spain and Sicily in the eleventh and twelfth centuries brought to Europe a new interest in Arabic philosophers, physicians and scientists. Indirectly, through Syriac and Arabic, Greek manuscripts were translated into Latin and European languages.

Alchemical explanation of the nature of matter was included in the treatises of such scholars as Arnold of Villanova (1240–1313), Roger Bacon (1214–94), and ALBERTUS MAGNUS (1193–1280). They contained not only mystical theory but also important practical recipes. Arnold of Villanova described distillation of wine; Roger Bacon gave a recipe for gunpowder and directions for constructing a telescope. The alchemist became a recognisable figure on the European scene, and kings and nobles often supported alchemists in the hope of increasing their resources. Frequently, however, alchemists who failed in their attempt to produce the promised gold lost their lives. In time, alchemy fell into disrepute because of the nefarious character of its practitioners. It is said that Frederick of Wurzburg maintained special gallows for hanging alchemists.

From the fifteenth to the seventeenth centuries, alchemical symbolism and allegory became increasingly complex. Practical alchemists turned from attempting to make gold towards preparing medicinals. A leader in this movement was Philipus Aureolus PARACELSUS. He was the first in Europe to mention zinc and to use the word alcohol to refer to the spirit of wine. After the scientific revolution in the seventeenth century, alchemy became marginalised and interest in transmutation became limited to astrologers and numerologists. Nevertheless, the chemical facts that had been accumulated by alchemists as a by-product of their search for gold became the basis for modern chemistry. In the West, interest in the spiritual dimension of alchemy was rekindled in the mid-twentieth century through the works of the Swiss psychiatrist Carl Gustav JUNG (1875–1961) on gnostic and alchemical spiritualism.

ALECTROMANCY

Derived from the Greek *alectruon* ('cock') and *manteia* ('divination'), this is a method of divination using a cock or hen which is placed in a circle of grain around which are placed letters of the alphabet. The letters close to where the bird pecks are gathered and assembled to answer specific questions. If a simple 'yes' or 'no' is required then only two piles of grain would be used.

ALEUROMACY

Derived from the Greek *aleuron* ('flour') and *manteia* ('divination'), this is a method of divination using flour. Sentences were written on slips of paper, each of which was rolled up in a little ball of flour. These were thoroughly mixed nine times and then divided among the participants, who would supposedly learn their fate. Another method used was sloshing out a mixture of flour and water from a bowl and interpreting the patterns of floury residue left on the bottom and sides.

ALGOL

A star in the constellation of Perseus, known as the evil or demon star (from Arabic *al ghul*, 'the demon').

ALL HALLOWS' EVE *see* HALLOWE'EN.

ALOMANCY

Derived from the Greek *halo* ('salt') and *manteia* ('divination'), this is a method of divination by interpreting random patterns using salt, probably following similar methods to ALEUROMACY.

ALPHA

The first letter of the Greek alphabet, representing a beginning, either the start of all things, or the commencement of a particular occult process. Often found in carved or inscribed signs, along with OMEGA.

ALPHITOMANCY

Derived from the Greek *alphitomantis* ('divination using barley'), this is a method of determining the guilt of a person by feeding him or her a specially prepared barley loaf. If the person suffers from indigestion, this is interpreted as a sign of guilt.

AMORC *see* ROSICRUCIANS.

AMULET

An object, image, drawing or inscription imbued with magical properties to ward off the EVIL EYE. Simple amulets are objects which have an odd shape or colour that catches the eye, or are very rare, such as a four-leaf clover. Amulets are often worn around the neck or as rings, especially in the form of jewellery. Virtually anything can become an amulet, depending on the different beliefs in different cultures. Some are designs or symbols on buildings, holy places and tombs. Semiprecious stones were particularly common as amulets, as were eyes; the best-known eye amulet being the ancient Egyptian EYE OF HORUS. Organic amulets, such as fruit, vegetables, berries, nuts and plants are also common in certain parts of the world, as in the use of garlic to ward off vampires. Various metals are also commonly ascribed amuletic powers against evil, for instance, iron is universally believed to guard against demons and witches. *See* TALISMAN.

ANATHEMA
A curse or denunciation, invoking God, normally applied from a Christian standpoint to an evil or heretical doctrine or person.

ANCIENT MYSTICAL ORDER ROSAE CRUCIS *see* ROSICRUCIANS.

ANGEL
An immortal spiritual being which acts as an intermediary between God and humanity. The word 'angel' is derived from the Greek *angelos* and the Roman *angelus* for 'messenger'. Most religions class angels as demons who may be friendly or unfriendly towards mankind, although in popular belief angels are good and demons bad. The legions of angels are ranked into varying orders, the most popular hierarchy is that described by Dionysius the Areopagite (early fifth century) in his *De Hierarchia Celesti*, which arranges them in three triads: 1. Seraphim, Cherubim, and Thrones in the first circle; 2. Dominions, Virtues, and Powers in the second circle; 3. Principalities, ARCHANGELS, and Angels in the third circle. Before the eighteenth century it was believed that angels regularly interceded in the affairs of human beings. With the Enlightenment, angels became the preserve of poets and romantic fantasy. Several leading figures in occult thought claimed to commune with angels during states of trance, including

the Swedish mystic Emanuel SWEDENBORG and the philosopher Rudolf STEINER. Many people still claim to experience angelic visions, especially those who have gone through so-called 'near-death experiences', where in many accounts an angel appears to guide the dying across the threshold of death.

ANGELICAL STONE
A stone used for SCRYING by Dr John DEE, astrologer to Queen Elizabeth I, who claimed that it was given to him by the angels Raphael and Gabriel. It is now lodged in the British Museum.

ANIMAL MAGNETISM
An organic magnetism equivalent to physical magnetism, a vital force that can be transmitted from one person to another and produce healing. The concept was advanced in the late eighteenth century by the Austrian doctor Franz Anton MESMER who developed various therapeutic techniques based on the concept. *See* AURA.

ANIMAL PSI
The apparent ability of animals to experience CLAIRVOYANCE, precognition (knowledge of the future using some form of ESP), TELEPATHY and PSYCHOKINESIS. There is no scientific evidence for this phenomenon and most evidence relating to animal psi is anecdotal. According to recent research there are five types of basic animal psi: the ability to sense impending danger; the ability to sense, at a distance, the death of, or harm being caused to, a beloved human; the ability to sense the impending arrival of an owner; the ability to find the way home through unfamiliar territory; and the ability of an ani-

mal that is separated from its owner to find its way over long distances to be reunited.

ANIMA MUNDI
The Latin term meaning 'Soul of the World', regarded by ancient philosophers as being the divine essence which embraces and energises all life in the universe.

ANTHROPOMANCY
Derived from the Greek *anthropos* ('man') and *manteia* ('divination'), this is a method of divination by raising the dead or from interpreting the movements in the entrails of dead or dying men. *See* NECROMANCY.

ANTHROPOSOPHY *see* STEINER, RUDOLF.

ANTICHRIST
The name of the demon who is supposed to precede the Second Coming of Christ, as mentioned in *Revelation, 13*. In the early Christian church the term was applied to the Roman Empire, and during the Reformation the Papacy became identified by Protestants with the Antichrist.

ANUBIS
An Egyptian god, jackal-headed, whose function is to lead the souls of the dead to the tribunal of the Underworld, which will judge whether they are worthy of entering.

APOLLYON
Greek name of ABADDON, a major demon, sometimes a form of Satan, like the spirit met by Christian in *The Pilgrim's Progress*.

APORRHETA

A Greek word relating to the esoteric instructions revealed to initiates during ceremonies in the Egyptian and Grecian MYSTERIES.

APPARITION

The supernatural manifestation of people, animals, objects or spirits. An apparition of a dead person is also called a ghost. Since the late nineteenth century there have been many studies of the phenomena, but conclusive proof of the existence of apparitions remains elusive. Reported experiences of apparitions usually involve strange smells, extreme cold and the displacement of objects. Some apparitions appear corporeal, others luminous or transparent. Ghosts are often clothed in period costume. Most apparitions appear for a specific reason, such as to deliver a warning, or to offer comfort for grieving relatives, or to impart essential information. In the 1980s a poll in the United States by the University of Chicago revealed that 42 per cent of the adult population and 67 per cent of widows reported experiences with apparitions of some form, either visual images, noises and voices, or an uncanny sense of a lingering presence.

APPORT

An object (such as a piece of jewellery, money, fruit or flowers, even live animals) which supposedly materialises out of nothing in the presence of a MEDIUM. During the height of SPIRITUALISM in the late nineteenth century, the production of apports, or 'apporting', was a common feature at seances – the live dove was a popular favourite. Most mediums said the objects were gifts from the spirits, but many were later exposed as frauds, being discovered with objects hidden in their clothing to produce just at the right moment during the seance, which were usually held in darkened rooms, making sleight-of-hand much easier. *See* SEANCE; MATERIALISATION.

AQUARIUS

The eleventh sign of the ZODIAC.

dates: 21 January to 18 February.

represented by: the water-carrier.

glyph and origin: there are several links with the water carrier, and the glyph clearly resembles water waves, although the similarity to serpents has also been noticed.

ruling planet and groupings: Uranus; masculine, fixed and air.

typical traits: Aquarians are renowned for their independence and the fact that they like to operate according to their own rules. This can lead to them becoming very stubborn, but they can be inspiring because they do not easily lose hope. Aquarians are friendly, although they may not be totally reliable when circumstances become difficult, and highly creative in terms of ideas. However, they are not necessarily sufficiently practical to see through the ideas. Overall, they may be a little perverse or paradoxical, but beneath it all is a gregariousness and a real wish to help.

family: because of their independence, Aquarians may find it difficult to establish an emotional tie. However, providing they find the right type, who is not weak but capable and sensible, personal relationships can be very successful. They are usually totally faithful.

With children, they are supportive but may find it difficult to cope with emotional problems. Children may be a little unconventional, and some school environments may not be conducive to the full development of their potential. On the positive side, children will be originators, naturally friendly, and show the Aquarian traits of creativity and an affinity for science. The natural friendliness should not, however, be allowed to develop into a trust of anyone, particularly strangers.

business: not surprisingly, Aquarians like the freedom to do whatever they want, and they tend not to heed anyone who tries to boss them around. They are highly inventive and are generally good with any subject of a technical nature. They are also highly competent at practicalities. This makes for a considerable range of occupations, and Aquarians often turn their hand to science, communications, teaching, social work and general administration.

wider aspects: Aquarians are by their very nature a little out on a limb and unconventional, but their very positive qualities make this an interesting Sun sign.

associations: *colour* – electric blue; *flowers* – orchid; *gemstone* – aquamarine; *trees* – fruit trees; *food* – a light diet is best, including fruits.

ARCANUM
In general the term means anything hidden, the plural 'arcana' being applied to all the esoteric wisdom of occult lore. The word is also used to denote any one of the twenty-two picture cards (the Major Arcana) of the TAROT pack.

ARCHANGELS
The name given to the incorporeal beings of the third circle

21

(Eighth Hierarchy), according to Dionysius the Areopagite (*see* ANGEL), the beings of the sphere of Mercury. The Archangels are said to guide the spiritual destiny of groups of people, of nations, rather than individuals (which is the role of angels); this probably explains why the Archangels are often pictured as carrying formalised models of cities in their arms. In Judaism and Christianity, the most important are the seven archangels each of whom is assigned one of the seven spheres of heaven: Gabriel, Raphael, Michael, Uriel, Joophiel, Zadkiel and Samael (SATAN).

ARIEL

The personalised name of a spirit said by the English dramatist Thomas Heywood (*The Hierarchie of the Blessed Angells*, 1635) to be one of the seven spirits of the waters. In John Milton's *Paradise Lost* (1667) he is one of the rebel angels, but William Shakespeare, who popularised the name in *The Tempest*, makes Ariel a SYLPH or air spirit. In the play he is first enslaved by the witch Sycorax, who exhausts his powers and then becomes the tormented plaything of her son, Caliban, before he is finally liberated by the magician Prospero.

ARIES

The first sign of the ZODIAC.

dates: 21 March to 20 April.

origin and glyph: the ram's horns, which may be traced back to Egypt.

ruling planet and groupings: Mars; masculine, cardinal and fire.

typical traits: Arians have several noticeable characteristics, such as courage, seemingly boundless energy, enthusiasm, initiative and enterprise, and a desire for adventure and travel. This means that when faced with a particular challenge, there is a tendency to rush in without heeding the consequences, and this can often cause problems. This impulsiveness is, of course, one of their less appealing traits, and it may also be accompanied by selfishness. This manifests itself in the need to accomplish set tasks and reach planned goals, although they tend to have the beneficial quality of being able to concentrate on the primary aim by removing anything that is unnecessary and of little importance. Competitiveness is never far from the surface for an Arian, no matter what aspect of life is involved.

family: in personal relationships, Arians can be very passionate, and Aries men look for a strong partner. Arian women are equally demanding and often prefer a career to being at home, although the two can be combined. If there are no adverse influences elsewhere on a chart, Arians are faithful but there are those who are continually moving on to new relationships and challenges.

Children of this sign tend to show the typical traits of liveliness and enthusiasm, but as there is always an underlying impatience, a child may soon lose interest and look for something new. Performance at school may be chequered because of this trait. However, should such a child lose his or her place or standing, his or her natural competitiveness and wish to lead usually reassert themselves, and lost ground is regained and held.

As parents Arians are, not unexpectedly, energetic and in the main will encourage their children in a variety of activities. It is all too easy, however, for the ebullience of the parent to overshadow the wishes of the child, and that can easily result in discord.

business: to satisfy the Arian character, an occupation ought to be challenging, with goals to aim for and with the opportunity to lead. Boring, routine jobs would not satisfy, but if that were the outcome then other activities would have to compensate. Large organisations with some freedom and a defined career structure, such as teaching, the police or the civil service, would be appropriate.

wider aspects: in their other pursuits, Arians import their eager approach, which in certain circumstances can be positively damaging, for example, knocks and bruises in the early years.

associations: *colour* – red; *flowers* – thistle, honeysuckle; *gemstone* – diamond; *trees* – thorn-bearing varieties; *food* – traditional rather than exotic.

ARIOCH

The name of one of the fallen angels in John Milton's *Paradise Lost* (1667) and is derived ultimately from the Hebrew meaning 'fierce lion' the name of a man in the Biblical Book of Daniel 2:14.

ARIOLATER

A diviner, a person who foretells the future from OMENS. The term is said to be from the Sanskrit *hira* ('entrails'), but some occultists trace its origin to the Latin *ara* (' altar'). *See* HARUSPEX.

ARITHMOMANCY

A term from the Greek *arithmos* ('number') and *manteia* ('divination'), relating to divination by numbers (*see* NUMER-

OLOGY). Esoterically it is concerned with the science of correspondences between gods, men and numbers, as taught by
PYTHAGORAS.

ASCENDANT
The degree of the ZODIAC which is nearest the eastern horizon
at the time of birth. This degree was originally called the
horoscopos in Greek astrology, from which the modern word
HOROSCOPE is derived.

ASHTORETH
The goddess of fertility and reproduction among the
Phoenicians, the equivalent of the Babylonian ISHTAR.

ASMODEUS
A DEMON who figures in the Apocryphal Book of Tobit as the
personal tormentor of Tobias's wife-to-be. The Hebraic name
Ashmedai (Destroyer) was probably from the Persian *Aesham-
dev*, the demon of concupiscence. In the *Testament of Solomon* Asmodeus reveals himself as the demon pledged to plot
against the newly wedded. The term 'flight of Asmodeus' is
derived from a work of literature by Le Sage (*Le Diable
Boiteux* 1707) in which Asmodeus takes Don Cleofas for a
night flight, and by magical means removes the roofs from
the houses of a village to show him the secrets of what passes
in private lives.

ASPECTS
An astrological term used to denote a large number of angular relationships between planets and other nodal points. The
various angles between planets and nodal points in a chart
have been invested with specific influences or powers which

work through the planets concerned. The traditional forms of astrology describe nine angular relationships only, these being divided into the major aspects and the minor aspects.

ASPORT
A term used of a psychic phenomenon involving the disappearance of an object from a location unhindered by physical barriers such as walls. Usually such a phenomenon allegedly occurs at a SEANCE, although it has also supposedly been observed during POLTERGEIST activities. *See* APPORT.

ASTARTE
Greek name of ASHTORETH, the powerful moon-goddess of the Phoenicians, and known by the Babylonians as ISHTAR. She wore a horned headdress, like the crescent MOON.

ASTRAGALOMANCY
A term derived from the Greek *astragalos* ('dice' or 'knucklebone') and *manteia* ('divination') and applied to a method of telling the future from the throw of dice or bones.

ASTRAL
The term appears to be derived from the Latin for 'star' and is sometimes applied to the stellar world as descriptive of the fabric of the heavens. In occult and astrological terminology the astral plane is contiguous in space (if not in time) with the material realm; it is the one which the spiritual part of a human being enters during periods of sleep and after death. The astral realm is one normally invisible to ordinary sight, yet it is the proper dwelling of the higher spiritual bodies of man.

ASTRAL BODY

A name given to the spiritual appearance of the physical body. The Astral Body is said by occultists and clairvoyants to be of a fine, highly luminous and vibrating nature, flooded with colours of indescribable beauty. Occultists regard the Astral Body as having an independent existence on the astral plane during periods when the physical body is asleep or when a person consciously indulges in astral travel. *See* OUT-OF-BODY EXPERIENCE, AURA.

ASTRAL PROJECTION *see* OUT-OF-BODY EXPERIENCE.

ASTRAL TRAVEL *see* OUT-OF-BODY EXPERIENCE.

ASTROLOGY

The pseudo-scientific study of the influence of the celestial bodies on the Earth and its inhabitants. Astrology appears to be one of the most ancient of the surviving occult sciences, and evidence of a highly sophisticated system in Babylonian and Egyptian cultures has survived. Popular astrology is concerned with the reading of a HOROSCOPE chart cast for the moment of birth – in some cases complex methods of progressing the planets of the birth chart enable the astrologer to predict the future for the person for whom the chart was cast. The chart is interpreted in terms of the influence of the zodiacal signs (*see* ZODIAC) and the various different powers which the planets possess in these signs. A variety of different house systems (*see* HOUSES) is linked with interpreting the directions in the person's life in which planetary and other influences will manifest themselves. The planetary effects are not considered only in terms of zodiacal placing (on the basis that Mars in Leo is different from Mars in Cancer, for example),

27

but also in terms of the angles which they may or may not hold to each other; this realm of astrology is the study of ASPECTS.

ATLANTIS

According to ancient myth, the name of the vast island-continent, and the many civilisations which flourished on it, before being destroyed in a cataclysm. There are numerous legends regarding Atlanteans and how their advanced civilisation was destroyed by their misuse of power. Over forty locations for the site have been identified around the globe, but no real evidence of its existence has been discovered.

The first account of Atlantis was given by Plato in various dialogues around 350 BC. Plato recounts the story of Egyptian priests who 200 years earlier had reportedly described Atlantis as a powerful island empire seeking to dominate the Mediterranean world more than 9,000 years before Plato's time. The island was supposedly larger than Libya and Asia Minor combined and had been located in the Atlantic Ocean, west of the Pillars of Hercules. Plato described the Atlanteans as a wealthy, successful, politically advanced and militarily powerful society. Their army was defeated by Athens and shortly afterwards an earthquake caused Atlantis to sink beneath the ocean. In the Middle Ages few doubted that Atlantis had existed. Many theories suggesting the exact location of the lost island have been advanced, and the nature of its utopian political system has been discussed extensively.

In the late nineteenth and twentieth centuries various occult theories emerged regarding the lost island race. Madame Helena P. BLAVATSKY, cofounder of THEOSOPHY, believed that the Atlanteans were descendants from another legendary lost continent, LEMURIA, and were the Fourth Root Race of all humans. She claimed that the information had come from the BOOK OF DYZAN, an allegedly Atlantean work that had survived and was now in Tibet. The philosopher and occultist Rudolf STEINER claimed to be able to access the akashic records (*see* AKASHA), which also described the Atlanteans as descendants of Lemurians. Some writers have speculated that the present-day American Indians migrated from the Old World to the New by way of Atlantis. Although traditional accounts of Atlantis have been proved false, some archaeologists speculate that the Atlantis legend may have originated with the volcanic eruption that destroyed a highly civilised Minoan town on the island of Thera in the Aegean Sea about 1450 BC.

AUGUR

A soothsayer or diviner. Originally the term was applied to the priest or religious official who interpreted omens from the flight, song and feeding of birds (etymologically connected with the Latin *avis*, bird'). From this also comes Augury, which means either the act of divining in this way, or the forecast made as a result.

AURA

The name given to a subtle envelope of vital energy which apparently radiates around natural objects, including human beings, animals and plants. The aura is invisible, but is seen by clairvoyants as a halo of light, although not all clairvoyants describe the auras of similar objects or people in the same way. Although the body does have a magnetic field – a biofield – it is far too weak to account for a light-emitting halo of energy and, aside from the accounts of clairvoyants, there is no scientific evidence that the phenomenon exists. Belief in the emanation of vital energy from the body was present in ancient Egypt, India, Greece and Rome. In the sixteenth century PARACELSUS discoursed on the ASTRAL BODY and its 'fiery' aura; the theory of ANIMAL MAGNETISM advanced in the late eighteenth century by Franz Anton MESMER prompted a variety of scientific experiments to try to isolate and identify the phenomena.

In the years before World War I Dr Walter Kilner at St Thomas's Hospital in London developed a method of viewing auras, which he claimed appeared as a faint haze around the body, using an apparatus which rendered ultraviolet light visible. He developed a theory of auric diagnosis of illness, from his observations of the correspondence between the appearance of the aura and patient health. Kilner's work was greeted with scepticism by the medical profession, and his work was interrupted by the onset of World War I. In 1939 Semyon Davidovich Kirlian, a Russian electrician, developed a technique which he claimed recorded the aura on film, but this technique remains controversial (*see* KIRLIAN PHOTOGRAPHY).

AUSTROMANCY
Divination by means of the winds and interpreting cloud shapes. *See* AEROMANCY.

AUTOMATIC WRITING
Writing executed by a MEDIUM whilst in a TRANCE or altered state of consciousness. Occultists believe automatic writing is the product of communication with a spiritual being; psy-

chical researchers believe it emanates from the writer's own subconscious, or perhaps through ESP. The writer is usually unaware of what is being written. Typically the process is much faster than ordinary handwriting and the script is larger and more expansive. Automatic writers have also produced mirror script and backwards writing, starting from the bottom right of the page and finishing at the top left. At the height of SPIRITUALISM automatic writing was common in seances, where it was adopted as a superior method of communicating with the dead than RAPPINGS or using a PLANCHETTE. Automatic writing was supposedly invaluable in the psychic excavations carried out at Glastonbury in the early twentieth century (*see* GLASTONBURY, GLASTONBURY SCRIPTS, PSYCHIC ARCHAEOLOGY). Automatic writing has also been used by psychologists and psychiatrists in the investigation and treatment of mental illness.

AVATAR
Derived from the Sanskrit word *aloatara*, which means 'descent', and used in Hinduism to denote a god who has descended, by way of an incarnation, into either mortal or animal form.

AVEBURY
A village in Wiltshire, southern England, 129 kilometres (80 miles) west of London, which is the site of Avebury Circle, one of the largest prehistoric ritual monuments of Britain. It consists of a circular enclosure surrounded by a huge ditch, originally 12 metres (40 feet) wide and 9 metres (30 feet) deep, and a large external bank, broken by entrances from the north, east, south and west. Inside the ditch are the re-

mains of a circle of one hundred standing stones, up to 4 metres (14 feet) high and 335 metres (1,100 feet) in diameter, the largest stone circle in Europe. Inside it are two smaller circles, about 98 metres (320 feet) across, with stones at the centre of each. All the stones, termed megaliths, are of local sandstone, called sarsen, which occurs as large boulders on the adjacent chalk downs. From the south entrance an avenue of paired standing stones, since destroyed but now partially restored, linked Avebury with the so-called Sanctuary, a double circle of stones located about 2.4 kilometres (1.5 miles) away, which was destroyed in the eighteenth century.

Avebury was built in late Neolithic times, about 2000 BC, probably by the Bronze Age Beaker People. Later the site was occupied by a Saxon village. Silbury Hill, the largest prehistoric mound in Europe, and Windmill Hill, site of a Neolithic causewayed camp, are nearby. Some occultists regard the area as a psychic power centre. The site has a long history as a centre of allegedly paranormal activity, including reports of APPARITIONS, eerie noises and strange lights. In the 1980s the locality was a major site for CROP CIRCLES.

AVESTA
The Zoroastrian equivalent of the Bible, dating from the fourth century AD, and consisting of the recorded sayings and writings of ZOROASTER. It is sometimes wrongly referred to as the Zend-Avesta.

AZAZEL
Described by Milton as the standard bearer of rebellious angels by this name (*Paradise Lost*, 1, 534). In Islamic demonology Azazel is a DJIN, who is cast from heaven for refusing to

worship Adam. His name was changed to EBLIS, which means 'despair'.

AXINOMANCY

A term derived from the Greek *axine* ('axe') and *manteia* ('divination') and applied to an obscure form of divination from the heating of an axehead in the embers of a fire. Another method recorded among the ancient Greeks is that of placing an AGATE stone on a red-hot axe; its motion is taken to indicate the identity of someone guilty of a crime. The term also covers other methods of prediction, or answering questions, by means of an axe.

B

BAAL
A creator god imported into the mythology of ancient Egypt during the Eighteenth Dynasty. Baal means 'god', 'lord', 'owner' or 'master' and was applied to the chief or ruler of one of the primitive groups of nameless deities.

BAALZEBUB *see* BEELZEBUB.

BACCHUS
In mythology the name of the Greek god of wine, associated with untrammelled pleasure and licentiousness; in esoteric circles (under his Grecian names of Dionysus or Atys) he is regarded as a solar resurrectional god who atones for sin.

BACKWARD BLESSING
The practice of saying the Lord's Prayer backwards. It is said to invoke the devil and is sometimes mentioned in accounts of the SABBAT as one of the numerous profanations. *See* BLACK MASS.

BACON, ROGER (*c*.1214–1292)

An English philosopher and alchemist, born in Somerset, who studied at Oxford and Paris, and was celebrated for his unorthodox experiments. His contemporaries gave hin the name *Doctor Mirabilis*, 'marvellous doctor'. He became a Franciscan monk, but was hounded and imprisoned by the Order, which disapproved of his enquiring and scientific approach. *See* BRAZEN HEAD.

BALNEUM MARIAE

Medieval Latin for 'Mary's bath', in French *Bain Marie*, the name given to a kind of double cooker used by alchemists in ALCHEMY. The inner pan is gently warmed by the water in the outer pan, which is the only part in direct contact with the flames. It is said that the name is derived from the gentleness of the heat, but it is more likely that the term is derived from the image of a source of spiritual heat (that is, Jesus) being nourished by water (Mary).

BANSHEE

One of the household spirits of certain Scottish Highland or Irish families; the creature is said to wail at the death of a family member. The word is sometimes used to denote a sort of DEMON, but in Nordic folklore the banshee is always benevolent. The word is supposed to be derived from the Old Irish *ben sidhe*, 'woman of the fairy folk'.

BAPHOMET

A name sometimes given to a supposed DEMON but almost certainly a corruption of the word 'Mohammed'. Accusations of the blasphemous worship of Baphomet were levelled at the ORDER OF THE KNIGHTS TEMPLAR in the fourteenth century.

BARBASON

The name of a DEMON mentioned by William Shakespeare alongside LUCIFER and Amaimon in *The Merry Wives of Windsor* (Act II, scene ii). The playwright may have obtained the demon from Reginald SCOT's *Discoverie of Witchcraft* (1584).

BASILISK

The mythical king of the reptiles (from Greek *basileus* 'a king') sometimes called a COCKATRICE, said to be hatched from a cock's egg by a serpent. It was supposed to kill merely by its glance.

BATH-KOL

A heavenly or divine voice announcing the will of God. Also the name of what was probably a method of divination among the ancient Jews. It is said that the first words uttered after the appeal to Bath-kol were taken as being oracular: the words in Hebrew means approximately 'daughters of the voice'.

BEELZEBUB *or* BAALZEBUB

Baalzebub probably means 'Lord of the High House' and refers to the Syrian BAAL. This title could only properly apply to Solomon in his temple, so the Jews changed the name to Beelzebub, which translates as 'Lord of Flies'. Beelzebub came to be regarded as the leading representative of the fallen gods; in Matthew, 12:24, he is mentioned as 'Prince of the Devils', and this appellation has stuck, even though Milton has him next in rank to SATAN (*Paradise Lost*, I, 79).

BELL, BOOK AND CANDLE
After ceremonial excommunication in the Catholic Church, the officiating ecclesiastic closes the book, throws the candle to the ground (thus extinguishing it in earth), and has the bell tolled as though for one who has died. It is said that the book symbolises the book of life, the candle symbolises the (lost) soul, and the bell is technically the PASSING BELL, representative in this case of the spiritual death.

BELL-MAN
A form of gargoyle found on country churches, a semi-human figure with a bell in each hand. This was a TALISMAN against witches, since witches were said to be unable to practise their arts when church bells were ringing in the vicinity.

BELOMANCY
DIVINATION using feathered arrows. Labels are attached to the arrows, and the advice or oracle tied to the one which travels farthest is taken as valid.

BELPHEGOR
Originally the Assyrian form of 'Baal-Poer', the Moabitish god associated with licentiousness and orgies. The name was later applied by medieval demonologists to a DEVIL. According to legend, Belphegor was sent from Hell by the other demons to find out if there really was such a thing on earth as married happiness. Rumour of such had reached the demons but they knew that people were not designed to live in harmony. Belphegor's experiences in the world soon convinced him that the rumour was groundless. The story is found in various works of early modern literature, hence the

use of the name to apply to a misanthrope or a licentious person.

BELTANE

The Celtic May festival, to celebrate the arrival of summer; from Old Gaelic words meaning the blaze-kindling. In Druidic times, two fires were lit, and the tribe's cattle driven between them, in a purificatory rite. In later times, young men would leap over the fires in tests or displays of energy and virility.

BERMUDA TRIANGLE

A mysterious area in the Atlantic Ocean where paranormal events are alleged to occur. The Bermuda Triangle is bounded by Florida, Bermuda and Puerto Rico. It is also called the Devil's Triangle, Limbo of the Lost, Hoodoo Sea and the Twilight Zone. Numerous planes and ships have vanished there without a trace, often in good weather or near a landing site or port. Just before disappearing, crews have made radio contact indicating that nothing was amiss. In rare instances missing ships have been found but without their crew or passengers.

It was named in 1945, after the disappearance of six Navy planes and their crews on 5 December, a sunny, calm day with ideal flying conditions. Prior to that scores of ships of all sizes reportedly had vanished in the area. Strange phenomena have been reported ever since Christopher Columbus's voyage to America in 1492. Other phenomena witnessed in the area include bright lights or balls of fire; sudden explosive red flares in the sky; and UFO activity. Aeroplane crew members have reported sudden power failures, instrument failures and their inability to maintain altitude. In the lore of fishermen, the Bermuda Triangle is inhabited by monsters that kidnap ships.

One theory is that unusual weather conditions are responsible, other theories propose that phenomena are caused by alignments of the planets, time warps that trap ships and planes, forces emanating from the unknown ruins of ATLANTIS or cosmic tractor beams sent from UFOs to kidnap ships and people. Sceptics claim misleading information and sensationalist reporting have created a false mystery, adding that most disappearances can be attributed to bad weather, abandonment or explainable accidents. They say that incidents that occur in the Triangle are automatically considered mysteries because of the legends.

BESANT, ANNIE (1847–1933)

English social reformer and theosophist, née Wood. She married Frank Besant, an Anglican clergyman, in 1867 but separated from him five years later because of doctrinal differences. She joined the National Secular Society and, with the atheist journalist Charles Bradlaugh, crusaded for free thought, birth control and women's rights. Besant was also a member of the socialistic Fabian Society.

A few years after her conversion (1889) to THEOSOPHY – a philosophical religious movement based on mystical insights – Besant went to India, where she spent the rest of her life. She founded the Central Hindu College at Varanasi in Uttar Pradesh and was politically active. For many years, beginning in 1916, she campaigned for Indian home rule. She also travelled extensively in Great Britain and the United States with Krishnamurti, her adopted son, whom she presented as a new messiah, a claim he later renounced. Besant wrote widely on theosophy and was president of the Theosophical Society from 1907 until her death.

BICORN
A mythical creature with demonic undertones. In medieval literature it is mentioned as a beast that grows fat through living on the flesh of faithful and enduring husbands. The equivalent 'female' version is the Chichevache.

BILOCATION
The appearance of a person in two distant places at once. The double may appear in solid or ghostly form, and usually acts strangely or mechanically and does not respond when spoken to. Bilocation is said to have been practised by many mystics, monks and other holy figures through the ages, including famous Christian saints such as St Anthony of Padua, St Ambrose of Milan and Padre Pio of Italy. *See* OUT-OF-BODY EXPERIENCES.

BIRDS OF OMEN
AUGURS classified birds as either good or bad; owls, crows and ravens were generally considered birds of ill omen. In Celtic occult lore, the sight of three ravens on the ground, especially from behind, was an indication of some disaster ahead. Magpies are also associated with WITCHCRAFT and omens of death. Among birds whose appearance is lucky are swallows and storks.

BIRTH STONES
Occult literature links a number of precious stones with each of the twelve signs of the ZODIAC. These associations are used in talismanic magic (*see* TALISMANS) and in the production of

AMULETS. The stones were said to transmit a specific hidden power when used to make seals. They were also sometimes worn unsealed as magnetic centres to attract their corresponding powers of the stars. The stones now identified with the signs are: Aries, bloodstone; Taurus, sapphire; Gemini, chrysoprase; Cancer, emerald; Leo, chrysolite; Virgo, cornelian; Libra, opal; Scorpio, aquamarine; Sagittarius, topaz; Capricorn, ruby; Aquarius, garnet; Pisces, amethyst.

BLACK ART
The term is thought to come from the confusion of the etymology of NECROMANCY with the Latin word *niger*, which means 'black'.

BLACK MAGIC
The conscious exercise of evil, the perversion of white MAGIC. In occult lore, white magic is concerned with expanding consciousness and improving the common good. Black magic is the selfish and squalid perversion of magical arts to achieve power in some form, destroy others, or for personal gain. *See* BROTHERS OF THE SHADOW.

BLACK MASS
The blasphemous parody of the Christian rite and defilement of holy substances alleged to occur during the witches' SABBAT. In the sixteenth and seventeenth centuries accusations of attendance at such devilish occasions became increasingly common. According to the theologians, demonologists and other self-appointed 'experts' on witchcraft, who derived their information from witchcraft confessions obtained by torture, the unorthodox ritual involved naked virgins on altars, BACK-

41

WARD BLESSING, the sacrifice of toads and chickens, the host being desecrated and made of noxious substances, the sprinkling of the congregation with urine instead of holy water and other such practices. *See also* SABBAT.

BLAVATSKY, HELENA PETROVNA (1831–91)

Russian-born American mystic and cofounder of the Theosophical Society. Born in Ekaterinoslav, she was married briefly in her teens to a Russian general but left him and travelled widely in the East, including Tibet. She supposedly exhibited psychic powers from an early age, and throughout her career claimed to perform feats of mediumship, LEVITATION, TELEPATHY and CLAIRVOYANCE.

She went to America in 1873, and in 1875, with Colonel Henry Steel Olcott, founded the Theosophical Society in New York (*see* THEOSOPHY) and later carried on her work in India. Her psychic powers were widely acclaimed and attracted many converts to theosophy, including ANNIE BESANT, whose home became the headquarters of the Theosophical Society in London. In 1885 the Society for Psychical Research published a damning report alleging fraud and trickery by Blavatsky and her associates. Her writings include *Isis Unveiled* (1877) and *The Secret Doctrine* (1888).

BOGY

The name given to a hobgoblin, probably derived from the Scottish word 'bogle' or from 'boggart'.

BOOK OF CHANGES *see* I CHING.

BOOK OF DYZAN

An Eastern occult text used by Madame Helena P. BLAVATSKY

as the basis for the commentaries which form the first book of her *Secret Doctrine* (1888). The text gives, by means of esoteric symbolism, the history of cosmic evolution.

BOOK OF THE DEAD
A collection of ancient Egyptian religious and magical texts concerned with ensuring the safe passage of the soul through Amenti (the Egyptian Hell).

BOOK OF THOTH *see* THOTH.

BORLEY
The rectory at Borley, Suffolk, was said to be the most haunted house in England. Although much of the evidence of spirits and POLTERGEISTS was manufactured by the fake psychic Harry Price, it is still believed by many that the house (which burned down mysteriously in 1939) was genuinely haunted, likewise the church close by, where the ghost of a nun has been seen.

BRAHAN SEER
The name given to Coinneach Odhar, who was born on the Isle of Lewis and lived in the Brahan area of Ross and Cromarty, Scotland, in the seventeenth century. Gifted with 'SECOND SIGHT' (the power of seeing things future or distant), he also had the aid of a magic stone. He is said to have forecast the railway train, the building of the Caledonian Canal and many other events. Most famously, he incurred the enmity of the Countess of Seaforth by reporting the scandalous doings of her absent husband. She had him burned alive in a tar barrel but not before he had prophesied the decline and fall of the Seaforths.

BRAZEN HEAD

A common theme of occult writings is that of the artifical head which can speak and which has supernatural knowledge. The English alchemist Roger BACON is said to have made one. While Bacon slept, it spoke three times to his assistant, one Miles, at half-hourly intervals: 'Time is', 'Time was', and finally 'Time is past', whereupon it broke into pieces.

BROCKEN

This peak in the German Harz mountains has many associations with magic and witchcraft. The Brocken Spectre is a ghostlike looming figure that is seen by walkers on misty days (*see* GREY MAN). On the summit of the hill is the *Hexentanzplatz*, or site of the witches' dancing ground. On Saint WALPURGIS Night, witches are said to assemble here for a night of festivity and wild dancing.

BROTHERS OF THE SHADOW

Sometimes also called the Dark Brothers or the Grey Brothers, terms used in occultism to denote those men and women who consciously choose to follow the practices and ethos of BLACK MAGIC, in what is called the Left-hand Path or the Path of Shadows. Their work is contrary to the work of white magicians, sometimes called 'Sons of Light', who are claimed to follow the pathway of evolution, self-perfection and self-sacrifice.

BULWER-LYTTON, SIR EDWARD (1803–73)

A prolific writer of the Victorian era, with a great interest in matters Occult. He wrote a life of PARACELSUS and a study of ROSICRUCIANISM. In his prophetic book *The Coming Race*, he introduced the concept of VRIL.

CABALA *see* KABBALAH.

CACODAEMON
The term means 'evil spirit' in Greek (*kakos daimon*) and was the name given by some medieval astrologers to the twelfth house of the horoscope figure. The inference that the twelfth house rules evil things, or the demonic element of the personality, is rejected by modern astrologers.

CADER IDRIS
This Welsh mountain, in Gwynnedd, is surrounded by occult legend. It is said to be the seat of a legendary giant, Idris, with a water-spirit dwelling in the lake, Llyn Cau, below the summit. Nearby is a crag known as the Devil's Rock.

CADUCEUS
The name given to a number of different symbolic wands, first appearing in ancient Mesopotamian cultures around 2600 BC, consisting of two serpents or BASILISKS twisted around a

rod. In Graeco-Roman mythology it was the white wand carried by Roman heralds suing for peace and the wand of Mercury (herald of the gods). Some occultists claim that the two entwined serpents symbolise the healing snakes of the demigod Aesculapius, and the symbol has been widely adopted as a symbol of the medical profession (a form of the caduceus is used in the badge of the Royal Army Medical Corps). In Hindu and Buddhist esoteric teachings the caduceus represents the two spiritual energies or healing forces that run up and down the human spine. For FREEMASONS the caduceus represents the harmony and balance between negative and positive forces, the fixed and the inconstant, the continuity of life and the decay of life.

CAGLIOSTRO, COUNT ALESSANDRO (1743–95)

An Italian adventurer and self-styled magician who became a glamorous figure in the royal courts of Europe where he reputedly excelled in various occult arts, such as PSYCHIC HEALING, ALCHEMY and SCRYING. His real name was Giuseppe Balsamo and he came from a poor family in Palermo, Sicily. At the age of twenty-three he went to Malta and was initiated into the Order of the Knights of Malta where he studied alchemy, the KABBALAH and other occult secrets. Later, in London, he joined the Freemasons, and subsequently spent his life roaming the royal courts in Europe performing various occult arts and peddling magic potions and an 'elixir of immortal life' with the aid of his beautiful wife, Lorenza Feliciani.

In 1785 he became involved with the 'Queen's Necklace Affair': he was set up by Countess de Lamotte who swindled 1.6 million francs for a diamond necklace – supposedly for

Marie Antoinette – and then accused Cagliostro of stealing it. He was sent to the Bastille and then tried for fraud. After his release he ended up in Rome, where he attempted to create an 'Egyptian Freemasonry' order. He was imprisoned by the church, questioned by the Inquisition and sentenced to death in 1791. His sentence was later commuted to life imprisonment by Pope Pius VI. After his death rumours that he had miraculously escaped and was still alive persisted for years throughout Europe, Russia and America.

CALIBAN
The name of the deformed half-human offspring of a devil and the witch Sycorax in Shakespeare's *The Tempest*. *See also* ARIEL.

CAMBION
A name given in the post-medieval period to the semi-human offspring of either an INCUBUS or a SUCCUBUS.

CANCER
The fourth sign of the ZODIAC.
dates: 22 June to 22 July.
origin and glyph: the glyph represents the breasts; Cancer probably came from ancient Babylon.
ruling planet and groupings: Moon; feminine, cardinal and water.
typical traits: the protective nature of the Cancerian is the overriding aspect of the character, but it is tempered by a stubborn and often moody streak. Although they tend to be of the worrying type, Cancerians have a remarkably good intuition, and their instinctive reactions and decisions can usually be relied upon. There is, however, a

changeability about Cancerians that manifests itself in several ways. They can rapidly adapt to pick up information, habits, etc, from others. It also means that they can be touchy and, like the crab, may be hiding a soft, easily hurt person beneath a seemingly hard shell.

family: the caring nature of Cancerians makes them excellent at building a home and good at forming long-lasting partnerships. In general Cancerians like to look back in preference to forwards and commonly stay in the same house for a long period of time. A slightly negative aspect is that their protective nature can become excessive and turn into clinging, and they may be touchy and occasionally snap for no apparent reason.

The sensitive almost retiring aspect of the character can be seen quite early in life, and this may continue to the point that they become very shy at school; they may hide behind a shell. It is commonly the case that Cancerians will eye new social contacts somewhat warily, keeping them at arm's length. However, when they get to know each other better, firm friendships can develop.

Cancerians usually like their extended family within a reasonably short distance and are keen to help anyone who may need their support.

business: Cancerians can turn their hand to most things, and their careful, intuitive approach can make them successful. They tend to work well with people and often adopt the role of mediator, where diplomacy is required. The caring professions (for example, medicine) are obviously well matched to the Cancer character, but teaching may also be suitable. Although business may prosper under a

Cancerian, there is often a tendency, even a fear, to change, which may show itself as inflexibility.

wider aspects: Cancerians are extremely sensitive, and while outwardly they appear charming and friendly, they can be temperamental and subject to wide mood swings. In general they love change, and while travel appeals, home has the greatest attraction.

associations: *colour* – silver and pastel shades; *flowers* – white flowers, especially the rose, lily; *gemstone* – pearl; *trees* – none in particular; *food* – dairy foods and fish.

CAPRICORN

The tenth sign of the ZODIAC.

dates: 22 December to 20 January.

origin and glyph: it may have originated with a mythical sea-goat from ancient Babylon. The glyph, is said to represent a goat's head and a fish's tail.

ruling planet and groupings: Saturn, feminine, cardinal and earth.

typical traits: it is said that there are two types of Capricornian, one of which has greater and higher hopes of life. In general, they are patient, practical and can be very shy, preferring to stay in the background – but, they are strong-willed and can stand up for themselves. Capricornians have a reputation for being mean, ambitious and rather hard people. A mean streak may often be directed at the self, and ambition, if tempered with realism and humour, can be positive. Usually the character is enhanced by other elements of the chart to produce a warmer personality.

family: Capricornians make good partners, although they

may come late to marriage to ensure a career has been established and that the correct choice is being made. Once set up, they are likely to be happy and to provide well, if economically, for the family. This aspect of caring can extend well outside the immediate family, and although there may be a lack of confidence, a Capricorn subject will not allow him or herself to be pushed around.

As parents, they can be too strict. However, they encourage their children and will make sacrifices to assist their child's progress.

Capricorn children may be a little slow to develop but usually come into their own eventually. They are very loyal and benefit from a secure background, which offers discipline, but at the same time they should be helped to build up their self-confidence.

business: although they make very good back-room people, Capricornians can make good leaders and do well in their own businesses. Many have an affinity for scientific work and pay attention to detail. They work well with people, although they tend to have an isolationist attitude, taking advice only grudgingly. One might well find them in local government, finance, publishing, building or politics.

wider aspects: those with Capricorn as their Sun sign are generally happy alone in leisure pursuits and therefore enjoy music, reading, etc.

associations: *colour* – dark colours; *flowers* – pansy, ivy; *gemstone* – amethyst; *trees* – pine, willow; *food* – starchy foods, meat.

CAPUT MORTUUM
The term in Latin means 'death's head' and was derived originally from ALCHEMY, where it was used to denote the residue after an alchemical operation such as distillation or sublimation.

CARTOMANCY
DIVINATION by means of playing cards. The most popular form of such divination is performed using the TAROT.

CELESTIAL BODIES
In occult teachings, the Sun, Moon and five planets (apart from Earth) known to the ancients, exercised great influence on earthly life and activity. Each had its own particular qualities and influences, and of course drove the astrological horoscope. The Sun, genuineness, nobility, authority; the Moon, instinct, needs, motherhood, the sea; Mercury, observation, communication, skill and knowledge; Venus, beauty, love, the arts; Mars, courage, warfare, competition; Jupiter, generosity, judgement, travel; Saturn, severity, age.

CENTURIES *see* NOSTRADAMUS.

CERBERUS
The three-headed dog of Greek mythology, which was the guardian of the gate to the infernal regions.

CERNE ABBAS GIANT
The huge outline of a naked giant cut in the chalk hillside above this Dorset village is an ancient fertility god. His erect phallus is 9.1 metres (29.8 feet) in length. The nearby earthwork known as the Trendle formed a meeting place where the

cult of the god was celebrated. Even today, women are said to make the seven times circuit of the figure in the hope of becoming pregnant.

CEROSCOPY
DIVINATION by means of melted wax, which is poured onto cold water to congeal. The diviner foretells the future from the various shapes of the hardened wax.

CHAIN OF BEING
The name given to an ancient belief in an immutable order in creation, ranging from the highest spiritual levels to the lowest inanimate objects on earth. This chain, or hierarchy, of beings is visualised as stretching as it were from the Throne of God to the very centre of the earth. Developed as a philosophical idea by Plato, added to by Aristotle, elaborated by the Neoplatonists, this has become a stock image underlying many philosophies and cosmological conceptions. Hell alone (because it had rebelled from the order of things) was not connected to this chain, yet the vision of Dante, resting as it did upon the redemptive thesis of theology, embraced even Hell in his view of the chain.

CHAKRA
A yogic term, derived from the Sanskrit for 'wheel', used to denote a series of circular vortices on the life force of a person, at which points energies are received, transformed and distributed. Chakras are believed to play an important role in physical, mental and emotional health, and in spiritual development. They are invisible to ordinary sight, but clairvoyants describe them as small depressions in the bodies of spiritu-

ally undeveloped persons but as larger coruscating and blazing whirlpools in more highly developed individuals.

CHANNELLING
The process by which a medium can communicate information from nonphysical beings, such as spirits, deities, DEMONS or aliens, through entering a state of TRANCE or some other form of altered consciousness. Channelling has existed in all cultures throughout history. In primitive societies a designated person – a priest, shaman, oracle or similar individual – had the responsibility of communicating with the nonwordly beings. The priestly caste of ancient Egypt communicated with the gods through trance; the ancient Greeks revered their oracles; the prophets and saints of Judaism, Christianity and Islam received the will of God in a form of channelling. In the nineteenth century, the claims of SPIRITUALISM to be able to communicate with the dead attracted a large following, and in the same period Madame Helena P. BLAVATSKY, cofounder of THEOSOPHY, claimed to be able to channel the wisdom of various Tibetan ADEPTS. Interest in channelling revived in the West during the 1970s and 1980s with the growth of the NEW AGE movement.

CHARM
Derived from the Latin *carmen* ('song'), this is a magical formula intended to be sung or recited to propitiate a spirit or to achieve some desired effect. The charm is often a part of the ritual involved in making an AMULET or TALISMANS.

CHEIROMANCY *see* PALMISTRY.

CHICHEVACHE *see* BICORN.

CHIMAERA
The Greek for 'she-goat', but in Greek mythology a monster with a goat's body, the head of lion and a dragon's tail.

CHINESE SYMBOLIC ANIMALS
The rich system of associations of the Chinese Twelve Earthly Branches (linked with the ZODIAC) has penetrated popular astrological lore in Europe mainly through the names of the associated symbolic animals in their so-called years.

Symbolic animal	*Zodiacal sign*
Rat	Aries
Ox	Taurus
Tiger	Gemini
Hare (cat)	Cancer
Dragon	Leo
Snake	Virgo
Horse	Libra
Sheep	Scorpio
Monkey	Sagittarius
Cock	Capricorn
Dog	Aquarius
Boar (pig)	Pisces

CHIROMANCY *see* PALMISTRY.

CHRISTIAN MYSTERIES *see* MYSTERIES.

CIRCLE *see* SEANCE.

CLAIRAUDIENCE

This means 'clear hearing' in French and is used to denote the faculty of supranormal hearing, that is, the perception of sounds, voices and music not audible to normal hearing. The phenomenon occurs in mystical and TRANCE experiences – shamans, prophets, priests, saints and mystics throughout history have been guided by clairaudient voices, usually interpreted as the voice of God, ANGELS, spirit guides or some other spiritual or divine essence. The ancient Greeks believed that DAIMONS, intermediate beings between human beings and the gods, whispered advice in the ears of men.

The Bible contains many episodes where God sends messengers to prophets and kings, and throughout history certain famous men and women, Joan of Arc, for example, are recorded as seeing visions and hearing voices of angels. Messages from the dead, perceived using the faculty of clairaudience, were a prominent feature of spiritualist seances (*see* SPIRITUALISM).

CLAIRSENTIENCE

This means 'clear sensing' in French and is the faculty of superphysical sense perception. It overlaps with other psychic abilities, such as CLAIRAUDIENCE and CLAIRVOYANCE, and is the psychic perception of smell, taste, touch, emotions and physical sensations, registered either internally or externally.

CLAIRVOYANCE

This means 'clear seeing' in French and is the faculty of supranormal sight, the ability to perceive objects or people that cannot be discerned through the normal senses. It overlaps with other psychic abilities such as CLAIRAUDIENCE,

CLAIRSENTIENCE, TELEPATHY, PSYCHOMETRY and REMOTE VIEWING. Clairvoyance normally requires some form of communication with the spirits or other nonphysical essences who give, or pretend to give, the desired knowledge. The ability has been acknowledged and used in all cultures throughout history – by prophets, fortune-tellers, shamans, wizards, witches and seers of all kinds. Western science began to investigate the phenomenon in the nineteenth century, when subjects treated by MESMERISM displayed clairvoyance and other psychic abilities. Since then a substantial body of evidence has been accumulated to support the existence of clairvoyance. As well as appearing to be a general ability among humans, it also appears to exist in animals (*see* ANIMAL PSI).

CLEIDOMANCY
Derived from the Greek *kleis* ('key') and *manteia* ('divination'), this term is applied to a large number of different methods of foretelling the future through the use of a key. One method involved writing a question on a key and placing the key in a Bible, which was then hung in such a way that permitted it to turn – the direction of the movement dictating the response. Another method involved placing the key in a clenched fist and allowing a pregnant woman to touch one of the two proffered fists. If she touched the one in which the key was held, then it was claimed that the child would be a girl.

CLEROMANCY
DIVINATION by means of dice. Sometimes the term was used to denote any method of divination involving the throwing of small objects like dice.

CLIMACTERICS

From ancient times it has been believed that certain years in the course of life are more liable to danger or change than others. The most important of the climacterics are the septenary years – 7, 14, 21, 28, etc – which are associated with lunar periodicities linked by such occultists as Madame Helena P. BLAVATSKY and Rudolf STEINER with the soul's growth.

CLOUD DISSOLVING

Making clouds disappear by concentration of thought and will. Claims that cloud dissolving is proof of the existence of PSYCHOKINESIS are rejected by most experts, who point out that small fair-weather clouds usually disappear of their own accord within about twenty minutes of forming. Nevertheless, psychic control over weather patterns – making the Sun appear, or making it rain – is an ancient skill claimed by shamans in many cultures around the world. In the United States, various American Indian tribes have rain dance ceremonies. How effective these ceremonies are remains unknown.

CLURICAUNE

In Irish folklore, an elf with evil tendencies. He has knowledge of hidden treasure and is the fairies' cobbler. He is the same as the LEPRECHAUN.

COCKATRICE

A mythical monster, sometimes used in heraldry. It has the wings of a bird, the tail of a dragon and the head of a cock, its name being derived from the belief that it was hatched from a cock's egg by a serpent. The power of its eyes is so terrible that its glance can kill. *See also* BASILISK.

COCYTUS
In classical Greek usage the name of one of the five rivers of Hell, along whose banks the unburied would wander for a century.

COLUMBA, SAINT (521–597)
A most curious episode is recorded in Adamnan's *Life of Saint Columba*, written from direct knowledge. Columba's follower, Oran, died and was buried in a chapel on Iona. But before the grave had been filled, the dead monk sat up and cried out that he had seen strange things, and that neither Heaven nor Hell were as they had been led to believe. Columba, horrified, called for earth to be thrown into the grave to stop Oran's mouth for ever.

CONAN DOYLE, SIR ARTHUR (1859–1930)
The creator of Sherlock Holmes took a keen interest in arcane subjects such as spiritualism, spirit photography, etc. The events he was most excited by, like the Cottingley 'FAIRY photographs' taken in 1917 by two young girls, Frances Griffiths and Elsie Wright, have subsequently turned out to be fakes by which Sir Arthur (and many others) had been fooled.

CONJURATION
The practice of raising spirits by means of carefully formulated rituals. These rituals take many different forms, many of them described in the GRIMOIRES, especially the *Grand Grimoire*, which contains probably the earliest printed account of the manufacture of PACTS with DEMONS.

CONTROL *see* MEDIUM.

CORAL

In ancient times coral was regarded as a TALISMANIC protection, even without the addition of pictures or symbols. It was used as a charm against whirlwinds, shipwreck and fire.

CROP CIRCLES

Large circular depressions or patterns that appear in the middle of grain fields when the crop is quite high. Most crop circles have been found in the southeast of England since the early 1980s but others have been reported in the United States and mainland Europe. Some have been exposed as hoaxes but others remain unexplained. Crop circles range in diameter from as small as three metres (ten feet) to over a hundred metres (315 feet). They appear overnight, and no tracks leading up to them are found, suggesting some external force from above is responsible. Some theories blame natural causes, such as freak weather conditions or excess irrigation; others claim that the depressions are made by UFOs or are communications from other intelligent life forces. As yet no conclusive evidence has been found for any of these theories.

CROWLEY, ALEISTER (1875–1947)

English magician and occultist, who described himself as the 'Beast of the Apocalypse' and was called by the media 'The Wickedest Man in the World'. Crowley both enraged and fascinated others with his rites of sex, magic and blood sacrifice. Despite his excesses, some consider him one of the most brilliant magicians of modern times.

He was born Edward Alexander Crowley in Leamington

Spa, Warwickshire. His parents, members of a fundamental-ist sect, the Plymouth Brethren, raised him in an atmosphere of repression and religious bigotry. He rebelled to such an extent that his mother christened him 'the Beast' after the Antichrist. Crowley was drawn to the occult at a young age and was fascinated by blood, torture and sexual degradation. He studied at Trinity College, Cambridge, but never earned a degree, instead devoting his time to writing poetry and study-ing occultism. In 1898, he joined the London chapter of the Hermetic Order of the Golden Dawn (HOGD) and quickly advanced to the highest grade. After leaving Cambridge he named himself Count Vladimir and pursued his occult activi-ties full-time in London.

Stories of bizarre incidents circulated, perhaps fuelled in part by Crowley's mesmerising eyes and aura of supernatu-ral power. Some individuals professed to see a ghostly light surrounding him, which he said was his astral spirit. His flat was said to be pervaded by an evil presence, and people who crossed him were said to suffer accidents. (This power was also claimed by Crowley's contemporary, the eminent novelist John Cowper Powys, although Powys feared and tried to subli-mate this 'gift' in himself).

Following his expulsion from the HOGD, Crowley travelled and delved into Eastern mysticism. He lived for a time at Boleskin Manor on the southern shore of Loch Ness in Scot-land. He had an enormous sexual appetite, and his animal vital-ity and raw behaviour attracted an unending stream of willing women. In 1903 he married Rose Kelly, the first of two wives, who bore him one child. He had a steady string of mistresses and also tried unsuccessfully to beget a child by magic, the ef-forts of which he fictionalised in a novel, *Moorzchild* (1929).

He spent World War I in the United States, putting out pro-German propaganda. In 1920, while driving through Italy, he had a vision of a hillside villa. He found the place on Sicily, took it over and renamed it the Sacred Abbey of the Thelemic Mysteries. Envisioned as a magical colony, the villa served as the site for numerous sexual orgies and magical rites, many attended by his illegitimate children. The behaviour led Benito Mussolini to expel Crowley from Italy in May 1923.

Crowley's later years were plagued with poor health, drug addiction and financial trouble. He earned a meagre living by publishing his writings. Much of his nonfiction is rambling and muddled but continues to have an audience. In 1934, desperate for money, he sued the sculptress Nina Hammett for libel in her biography of him, *Laughing Torso* (1932), in which she stated that Crowley had practised black magic and indulged in human sacrifice. The testimony given at the trial so repulsed the judge and jury that the trial was stopped and the jury found in favour of Hammett.

In 1945 Crowley moved to a boarding house in Hastings, where he lived the last two years of his life, dissipated, drug-addicted and bored. Crowley's published books include *The Book of the Law* (1904), *Magick in Theory and Practice* (1929) and *The Book of Thoth* (1944).

CRYSTAL GAZING *see* SCRYING.

CTHULHU
Although the invention of a modern author, Howard Phillips Lovecraft (1890–1937), this has become the centre of a quasi-occult school. Lovecraft was a novelist of the macabre and the evil. His Mythos was a brood of sub-demonic creatures of

his creation, Cthulhu, Yuggoth, Yog-Sothoth, and others. Lovecraft detested modern scientific civilisation and re-created a world of magic, horror and mystery in which nameless dread is constantly lurking at the corner. He wrote, 'We live on a placid island of ignorance in the midst of black seas of infinity, and it was not meant that we should travel far.' He believed that science was made up of separate fields of knowledge, with ever-more dangerous gaps opening up between them, while magic was a unity. His books are largely unread, but his ideas, and his creations, live on.

CURSE DOLLS
Figurines of wax or clay, intended to represent a person, and usually incorporating something taken from that person, like a hair, so that the maker can do harm to him or her by doing harm to the figurine. *See also* POPPET.

CURSING
To put a curse on someone was a clear demonstration of occult power. It is an ancient practice, the purpose of which was to mark out someone who had strayed from the path of proper thinking or incurred the enmity of the priest, witch or magician (*see* ANATHEMA). The effectiveness of a curse has always been in direct proportion to the subject's awareness of its existence. To be singled out and condemned in public had a tremendous mental impact. Equally, to know that someone had possession of a piece of clothing, or hairs of one's head, with malevolent intent, might be enough to bring on the desired effect.

Some locations have been believed to be protected against entry or robbery by a curse. The death of Lord Carnarvon soon after he entered the newly found tomb of Tutankhamun in 1922 led to speculation on the 'curse of Tutankhamun'. Undoubtedly the Pharaoh's tomb, like all others, would have been protected by many magic spells.

CRYSTALOMANCY *see* SCRYING.

DACTYLIOMANCY

Derived from the Greek *dakterlios* ('finger ring') and *manteia* ('divination'), this term applies to a number of methods of divining the future with the aid of rings. Sometimes a ring is used as a pendulum, at other times it is dropped into a bowl of water, its position at the bottom determining the prediction or the response to a formulated question.

DAEDALUS

This legendary Greek figure is the source of more than one occult tradition. He constructed the Cretan LABYRINTH, where the Minotaur was concealed. He was the first man to fly, using wings of wax and feathers, and is said to have been the inventor of such basic tools as the saw and the axe.

DAIMON

The Greek *daimon* means 'divine power', 'fate' or 'god'. To the Greeks, daimons were intermediary spirits between human beings and the gods, acting as spiritual advisers.

DEAD SEA SCROLLS *see* GNOSTICISM.

DEATH CHART
A horoscope figure constructed for the date or time of death and interpreted by analogy with the birth chart of ASTROLOGY.

DEATH PANORAMA
A term sometimes used to denote the OUT-OF-BODY EXPERIENCE of the newly departed soul after death. According to occultists, when the ETHERIC BODY has finally separated itself from the physical shell the newly departed spirit contemplates a panoramic view of its preceding life for a period of approximately two or three days. What was before experienced sequentially, spread out in time, is now perceived as timeless (that is, in eternity) and viewed as a panoramic whole.

DEATH PRAYER
This term has two different senses. First, in regard to 'praying for the dead', the death prayer is used either to help the departed soul in the spiritual abode or to request help from such souls on behalf of the living. Secondly, the term is used to describe a special technique designed to deprive a person or persons of life. The ability to command DEMONS to kill the living is supposedly one of the most terrible powers of black magicians. It is a technique widely practised by witch doctors in primitive tribes and is one for which the VOODOO cult in particular has gained a certain notoriety.

DEE, JOHN (1527–1608)
English mathematician and astrologer, who was adviser to Queen Elizabeth I on occult matters. In 1555, during the reign of Mary Tudor, Dee was imprisoned briefly under suspicion

of using enchantments against the queen. It seems that Elizabeth I held him in high regard, although Dee himself appeared to have little or no psychic ability. He claimed to be able to communicate with angelic beings and to be skilled in SCRYING, but he actually employed seers to transcribe alleged angelic communications for him. *See* ANGELICAL STONE.

DEMIURGE
A spiritual creative force that is not the Supreme Being. The gnostics (*see* GNOSTICISM) proclaimed Jehovah a demiurge rather than all-powerful creator.

DEMOGORGON
Once a most secret name, first mentioned by Lactantius, a fourth-century Christian writer. It was the chief power of Hell, the very mention of the name of which was to invite disaster.

DEMON
A low-level spirit that interacts with the material world. The term 'demon' is derived ultimately from the Sanskrit root *div* ('to shine'), through the Greek *daimon* ('divine power'). To the Greeks daimons were intermediary spirits between humans and the gods (*see* DAIMON). In Western religion and occult lore, demons are classified into various elaborate systems and hierarchies of hell, and have ascribed to them various characters, forms, attributes and duties. The most complex hierarchy was devised by Johann Weyer, who estimated that there were 7,405,926 demons serving under seventy-two princes. In Christianity, demons are associated only with evil. They include those demons who were cast out of heaven together with LUCIFER, as well as pagan deities branded as demons by the church.

Demons devote themselves to tormenting human beings, assaulting them, sexually abusing them and possessing them. The possibility of sex with demons was denied before the twelfth century, but by the later Middle Ages belief in sexually voracious demons in alluring male or female form who preyed on sleeping men and women (*see* INCUBUS, SUCCUBUS) had become widely accepted. In the sixteenth and seventeenth centuries in Europe witches were regularly accused of having sex with demons (*see* SABBAT). It was held that demons could be expelled or kept at bay by the ritual of EXORCISM or by the use of certain prayers or a special CHARM, or by wearing an AMULET or TALISMAN. *See also* GRAND GRIMOIRE, GRIMOIRES.

DEMONIC SINS
According to demonologists, seven demons had specific control over each of the seven deadly sins, with the powers of inducing men and women to commit these. The demons and associated sins were: LUCIFER, pride; MAMMON, avarice; ASMODEUS, lechery; SATAN, anger; BEELZEBUB, gluttony; LEVIATHAN, envy; BELPHEGOR, sloth.

DEMONOMANCY
DIVINATION with the aid of DEMONS. It may be argued that all divinatory techniques are done with the aid of spirits and that virtually all popular methods of foretelling the future work through the agency of certain demons.

DEUTEROSOPHIA
A term for SECOND SIGHT, from the Greek words for 'second' and 'wisdom'.

DEVA

In Hinduism and Buddhism, a group of exalted spiritual beings or gods. The term 'deva' is derived from the Sanskrit for 'shining one'. In Hinduism there are three kinds of devas: spiritually superior mortals, those who have achieved enlightenment, and Brahman in the form of a personal god. In Buddhism, devas are gods who reside in heaven as a consequence of their good deeds. In occultism, the term deva is applied to a variety of celestial and infernal beings. Madame Helena P. BLAVATSKY introduced the concept of devas to the West, defining them as types of ANGELS or gods who were progressed entities from a previous planetary period. They arrived on Earth before humans and would remain dormant until a certain stage of human evolution was reached. More recently the term has been applied to NATURE SPIRITS, who may elect to help people. They usually are invisible but may be seen by CLAIRVOYANCE.

DEVIL

The word 'devil' appears to be derived ultimately from the Sanskrit root *div*. In its strictly Biblical sense the word is derived from translating the Hebraic 'Satan' into the Greek 'Diabolos', although SATAN was not directly an evil or fiendish being so much as a tester of man's relationship to God. In this way the two distinct beings, Satan and Diabolos, were first confused and then later merged. Later linguistic changes linked the Devil with 'DEMON', although in Greek the latter was not an evil being at all (*see* DAIMON). The Devil himself – the theologically conceived supreme embodiment of evil – has taken on many related names in this babel of confusion, such as BEELZEBUB, ASMODEUS, ABADDON, Behemoth, Belial and even LUCIFER. The classical image of the demonologists is derived from early patristic writings of the fourth century, which merged pagan elements (such as the half-bestial Pan) with a semi-human form, so what in Medieval times was sometimes pictured as almost a cartoon figure of fun became a sort of hierarchic great god Pan, with cloven hooves, goat head and a curiously anthropomorphised form. Yet in spite of this development of imagery, the forms (as indeed the names) of the Devil have remained more or less legion, in that he accommodates into his single being many of the forms of the lesser devils.

DEVIL'S MARK

The name given originally to a scar, birthmark or other blemish on the skin, said by witch-hunters and demonologists to have been imprinted by the Devil as a mark or seal of his possession of the person. In some early reports the Devil's mark (the *stigmata diaboli*) was sometimes confused with the witchmark, which was, properly speaking, a protuberance on the body, such as a wart or a mole, regarded by witch-hunters as a supplementary teat at which familiars and demons might suck. The finding of such demon imprints as Devil's marks or witchmarks became an important business of the expert PRICKING that preceded many witch persecutions. Devil's marks and witchmarks were said to be insensitive to pain, and the pricking of pins into such areas was supposed to draw no blood.

DEVIL'S TRIANGLE *see* BERMUDA TRIANGLE.

DIONYSUS *see* BACCHUS; MYSTERIES.

DIVINATION
The art of foretelling the future, finding the lost and identifying the guilty by using a wide range of techniques involving the conscious or unconscious use of spirit beings. The art has existed throughout history and in all cultures. It is usually the responsibility of a priest, prophet, oracle, witch, shaman, witch doctor, psychic or other person with claimed supernatural powers. Techniques fall into two main categories: the interpretation of signs, omens, portents and lots, and direct communication with the spiritual world through visions, TRANCE, dreams and possession. *See* ASTROLOGY, AUGUR, DOWSING, I CHING, OMEN, ORACLE, PROPHESY, TAROT.

DJIN
An Arab term usually translated as meaning approximately ELEMENTALS, although the djin are fearsome and usually portrayed as monstrous DEMONS. It is likely that the word GENII comes from *djin*.

DOUBLE
An exact replica of a person in the form of an APPARITION. They are usually encountered in a location distant from the actual person. They may act strangely or move mechanically (*see* BILOCATION). In occult lore, a double is a projection of the 'astral body' and is often associated with the imminent death of the person. In Irish lore, a double is called a 'fetch', in Germany it is *doppelganger,* meaning 'double walker'. It is possible to see one's own double, as did the English poet Percy Bysshe Shelley, shortly before his death by drowning. *See also* WRAITH.

DOWSING

An ancient form of DIVINATION using a forked stick, bent wire or pendulum to locate people, objects and substances. The technique can be used to find underground water, minerals, oil, pipes and cables. It is also used to locate lost objects, missing persons and murder victims, and to diagnose illnesses. The ancient Egyptians and Chinese used dowsing, and during the Middle Ages in Britain and Europe it was a common technique for finding coal deposits. It is not clear how dowsing works. When the dowser finds the right location, the dowsing stick begins to twitch in the dowser's hand, sometimes violently.

Dowsing is perhaps the only form of DIVINATION in regular general use outside the field of the occult. The notion that divining rods somehow pick up vibrations from earth force fields does not explain the ability of those who use maps in their homes, far away from the actual field sites. In World War I dowsers were used by the army to help find mines and unexploded shells. Dowsing rods were used by American troops in Vietnam to locate mines, buried mortars and booby traps. Some oil, gas and mineral companies use dowsers to complement conventional geological analysis. The pendulum technique is often used for diagnoses in alternative medicine. The pendulum is suspended over a patient's body, changes in its movement and rotation indicating healthy or unhealthy areas.

DRACULA

The name of a VAMPIRE in the novel of that name by Bram Stoker, published in 1897. Because of the popularity of this book, the term 'Dracula' is often now used to denote a vampire.

DRUIDS

Members of the ancient pre-Christian Celtic priestcraft of Britain and Gaul, a secret order about which almost nothing is known. The term 'druid' means 'knowing the oak tree' in Gaelic; the oak tree was sacred to the Celts. The Romans tell us that the Druids were magicians, but the nature of their magic is unknown. The Romans also tell us that they believed in the transmigration of souls (which may have been reincarnation). They are said to have conducted their cult practices in sacred oak groves, where one of their chief rites was harvesting mistletoe using a golden sickle. They are also thought to have offered human sacrifices, both by burning (their victims enclosed in giant human-shaped wicker frames) and by ritual throat-cutting. It is probable that they were the representatives of the ancient Nordic and Christian MYSTERIES.

The theory that the Druids built STONEHENGE or AVEBURY, advanced by some antiquarians in the seventeenth and eighteenth centuries, has been proved by modern archaelogical techniques to be false: the stones of both are vastly older than the Druid period.

In the ancient world, the Druids had a reputation for PROPHECY and DIVINATION. Various Druid groups flourish in Britain and the United States but claim no connection with ancient Druids. They celebrate eight pagan festivals in outdoor henges and groves, the most important being the summer solstice. Since 1985, modern Druids have been prevented from gathering at Stonehenge for the solstice, because of vandalism by spectators. American Druids use a replica of Stonehenge in Washington State.

DYBBUK *see* POSSESSION.

EBLIS

The demon AZAZEL, after being thrust from Heaven, is re-named Eblis and becomes the ruler of the devils. The word 'eblis' means 'despair'.

ECTOPLASM

A white, viscous substance with an ozone-like smell, which is said to exude from the orifices of MEDIUMS and is moulded by spirits to assume physical shapes. It has frequently been photographed in such a form, but the existence of the substance has never been proved. In fact the distinctive texture and smell of ectoplasm can be created using various ingredients, such as a mixture of soap, gelatin and egg white. In the late nineteenth century many fraudulent mediums used muslin. *See also* MATERIALISATION, SPIRITUALISM

EGYPTIAN DAYS

A series of calendrical lists of fortunate or unfortunate days, said to have originated from Egyptian astrological practices but probably derived ultimately from Assyrian sources. The Egyptian days are sometimes called the 'Lucky and Unlucky Days'

ELECTIONAL ASTROLOGY
The casting and interpretation of astrological charts to determine suitable times for commencing any specific activity, such as marriage, travel, commerce, and so on. This system was used by the astrologer Joan Quigley on behalf of President Ronald Reagan of the United States in the 1980s.

ELEMENTALS
The beings associated with each of the four ELEMENTS. Fire, the SALAMANDER; Earth, the GNOME; Air, the SYLPH; Water, the UNDINE.

ELEMENTS
The four basic elements of astrology are Fire, Earth, Air and Water. These support the material world but are not part of it, being spiritual principles. In occult lore, the signs of the elements combine to form the six-pointed star or SEAL OF SOLOMON.

ELEUSIAN MYSTERIES *see* MYSTERIES.

ELIXIR
A term derived from ALCHEMY and used to denote the supposed liquid, a draught of which would give eternal life or some similar required extension or intensification of being. While in popular imagination the Elixir is regarded as being a liquid, the early alchemical manuscripts also of-

ten describe it as a powder. The origin of the term is probably Arabic, for a word of similar sound denotes a powder used for healing wounds. Sometimes it was believed that the Elixir was the so-called PHILOSOPHER'S STONE, which could be used to turn base metals into gold or silver.

ELONGATION
In a psychic context the word is used to denote the elongation of the body of the MEDIUM in response to spiritual control. The famous Scottish medium Daniel Dunglas HOME, who was never exposed as a fraud, was reportedly seen to elongate almost as much as twenty-five centimetres (ten inches) during a SEANCE.

EMERALD TABLE
A legendary object, a tablet of emerald, engraved in Phoenician script by HERMES TRISMEGISTUS, with a message of secret and immense import. A Latin version of it was available around the year 1200, translated from Arabic. Its opening sentence ran: *Quod superius est sicut quod inferius et quod inferius est sicut quod superius ad perpetranda miracula rei unius,* 'that which is above is like that which is below, and that which is below is like that which is above, to achieve the marvels of the one thing'. This phrase, shortened into 'as above, so below', underlies all ASTROLOGY and much magical practice.

ESP (EXTRASENSORY PERCEPTION)
Extrasensory perception (ESP) means the ability to perceive information without the benefit of the senses. Such perceptions, collectively called PSI phenomena, are grouped in four main categories: TELEPATHY or mind-to-mind communication;

CLAIRVOYANCE or the awareness of remote objects, persons or events; precognition or the knowledge of events lying in the future; and retrocognition or the knowledge of past events in the absence of access to information about those events. Scientific theory does not recognise modes of perception other than those mediated by the sense organs and other body systems, so ESP by definition lies outside the realm of scientific explanation. Claims for the occurrence of ESP therefore remain controversial, although the converse condition also holds, that the existence of ESP cannot positively be disproved. In the twentieth century, attempts at controlled study of ESP phenomena have been undertaken by various persons and groups (*see* PARAPSYCHOLOGY). Such researchers often claim that ESP experiences can be induced by hypnosis, chemicals or other artificial means, so that they can be measured precisely under laboratory conditions. The scientific community as a whole does not accept ESP research reports because it does not find them verifiable or reproducible. Parapsychologists and others, however, maintain that ESP exists and should be explored even should it remain beyond the bounds of scientific understanding.

ETHERIC BODY
A term used by occultists to denote the sheath of vital forces that permeates the physical body. It was called by the philosopher and occultist Rudolf STEINER the 'Body of Formative Forces' and in some occult systems the etheric DOUBLE. *See also* AURA.

EVIL EYE
In WITCHCRAFT and BLACK MAGIC it is said that certain indi-

viduals have the power to cast evil spells or to project evil thought forms merely by looking at another person. The idea of this evil power is virtually universal, and there exists in virtually every language an equivalent term. For example, the *boser Blick* in German, *malocchio* in Italian, *mauvais oeil* in French. The English 'fascinate', which was originally connected with such ideas as binding by means of diabolical powers or pact was derived from the Latin *fascinum*. The fact of the evil eye has given rise to numerous protective devices against it. These include a wide range of magical signs and AMULETS, reflective surfaces, and, in particular, a number of obscene or phallic figures and amulets that are intended to deflect evil – such as the *corno*, a curved horn, and the curious gesture involving a clenched hand with the thumb stuck through middle and fourth fingers. Images of eyes are also used to avert evil (*see* EYE OF HORUS) on the grounds of SYMPATHETIC MAGIC, and many of the more ancient gems and symbols are designed with this in mind.

EXORCISM

The expulsion of troublesome evil spirits, ghosts or demons by special rites. These rites exist in many cultures and societies where spirits are believed to interfere with the mental, physical and spiritual health of human beings. Exorcisms are normally performed by an appropriate official trained in the necessary skills, such as priests or an occult ADEPT. The magical arts of exorcism involved ceremonial magic, and the official exorcism rites of Christianity are in many ways similar. This is one aspect of belief where orthodox religion and arcane cults meet head-on, and the conjunction is often stormy and violent. Ritual techniques include the use of ADJURATION, prayers, invective, incense, foul odours and the use of holy substances such as sacred herbs, blessed water or salt. In Roman Catholic rituals, exorcism is treated as a virtual tug-of-war with the possessing devil for the victim's soul. Certain symptoms of possession are supposed to manifest themselves before the exorcism can take place, such as LEVITATION, superhuman strength, speaking in tongues or CLAIRVOYANCE. Once exorcism commences, the victim suffers a violent sequence of fits, painful contortions, vomiting and swearing. Among Protestant churches, the Pentecostalists, charismatics and 'televangelists' often use the laying on of hands to 'drive out devils' and allegedly cure illnesses.

EXTISPICY

DIVINATION by means of entrails. This was probably the most frequent form of divination in the ancient world, although after the Roman period it fell largely into disuse in the West. The liver and intestines were the parts most closely examined. There is an ancient Babylonian clay model of a lamb's liver, divided into fifty-five separate zones of significance. The origins of the practice may lie in a primitive form of autopsy practised by pastoral tribes: if the animals' insides showed signs of ill-health, it was time to move on. The extispices of the Roman religious colleges were the *aruspices* or augurs. *See* HARUSPEX.

EXTRASENSORY PERCEPTION *see* ESP.

EYE OF HORUS

The highly stylised eye of the falcon-headed solar and sky god Horus (the Latin version of *Hor*) is associated with regeneration, health and prosperity. It was very common as an AMULET in ancient Egypt. Horus, the son of Osiris and Isis, was called 'Horus who rules with two eyes'. His right eye was white and represented the Sun; his left eye was black and represented the Moon.

According to myth, Horus lost his left eye to his evil brother, Seth, whom he fought to avenge Seth's murder of Osiris. Seth tore out the eye but lost the fight. The eye was reassembled by magic by Thoth, the god of writing, the Moon and magic. Horus presented his eye to Osiris, who experienced rebirth in the Underworld.

As an amulet, the Eye of Horus has three versions: a left eye, a right eye and two eyes. The eye is constructed in fractional parts, with $\frac{1}{64}$th missing, a piece Thoth added by magic. The Egyptians used the eye as a funerary amulet for protection against evil and rebirth in the Underworld, and decorated mummies, coffins and tombs with it. The BOOK OF THE DEAD instructs that funerary eye amulets be made out of lapis lazuli or a stone called *mak*. Some were gold-plated. Worn as jewellery fashioned of gold, silver, lapis, wood, porcelain or carnelian, the eye served to ensure safety, to preserve health and to give the wearer wisdom and prosperity.

FAIRY

The name given to a wide variety of supernatural beings that either help or hinder mankind. Fairy beliefs are strongest in the Celtic lore of Britain, Ireland and Europe. The word is derived from the Latin *fata*, 'fate', which refers to the mythological Fates, three women who spin and control the threads of life. According to theory, fairies are either earthbound unbaptised souls, guardians of the souls of the dead, ghosts of venerated ancestors, fallen ANGELS condemned to remain on earth, NATURE SPIRITS, or small human beings. They are said to have magical powers and to consort with witches and other humans with supernatural powers. They have many different names and come in all shapes and sizes. They are invisible and can only be seen by clairvoyants or when they make themselves visible. Sir Arthur Conan DOYLE was deeply interested in SPIRITUALISM and psychic phenomena. In the early 1920s he was fooled by a photograph purporting to show tiny, winged, female figures dressed in fashionable gowns and floating in the air. The picture was taken by two young sisters, Elsie and Francis Wright, of Cottingley, Yorkshire. The girls insisted the photograph was genuine, and, despite expert testimony that the picture was a fake, Doyle wrote about the picture as proof of fairies in his *The Coming of the Fairies* (1922). The Wright sisters did not admit that the photo was a fraud until the 1980s.

FAKIR

In India, a type of holy man, generally called a *sadhu*, who lives by begging and is supposedly capable of various magical and miraculous feats. Many of these tricks are produced using sleight-of-hand and cleverly designed props. Some of the more spectacular feats, such as lying on a bed of nails, immersing the limbs in hot ash and being 'buried alive', require yogic training involving breath control and meditation to induce trance-like states that suppress normal physical responses. The term *fakir* is from the Arabic word for 'poor'. In Islamic cultures the fakir renounces the material world and follows Allah as a beggar.

FAMILIAR

According to English WITCHCRAFT handbooks of the early seventeenth century (familiars do not appear in Continental witchcraft trials and literature), the name given to spirits attendant upon witches or magicians. Usually familiars are visible to ordinary sight, as, for example, in the form of dogs or cats, but in some cases it was claimed that witches were followed by a swarm of invisible familiars. The word is from the Latin *familiares*, but alternative Roman names were *magistelli* and *martinelli*, while the Greeks called them *paredrii*. It was held that the familiar, usually in the form of a small domestic animal, was given to the witch by the Devil as a companion, helper and adviser, which could be used to perform malicious errands, including murder and other feats of BLACK MAGIC.

FASCINATE

A term derived from the Latin *fascinare* ('to enchant') and used as a general term for the act of casting spells or (in particular) of throwing the EVIL EYE on another person. In late-Medieval literature a person 'fascinated' was usually under the spell of a magician or witch.

FATAE *or* FATES

Greek and Roman mythologies include three spiritual beings called in Greek the *Moirai*, in Latin *Parcae* or *Fatae*, who were supposed to control the destiny of a person. They were named (probably after Hesiod) Clotho, who held a distaff on which was the material of life; Lachesis, who spun the thread from this material; and Atropos, who made that final cut of the thread which ended life. Sometimes the three are called the Harsh Spinners, even though they do not all spin. Their 'spinning' was said to take place at birth, and in some periods also at marriage, when a new life or fate was made. The general word *moirai* means 'share' or 'apportioned lot'. *Lachesis* means approximately 'obtaining by lot' and *atropos* 'irresistible'. The three witches in Macbeth have been linked with these three spinners, from the old English term *weird*, which means approximately 'destiny'; the three 'weird sisters' were the Fates who control destiny.

FAUST *or* **FAUSTUS, DR JOHANN** (died c.1538)

Dr Johann Faust or Faustus was a German magician and astrologer who died around 1538. The legend of the man who made a pact with the DEVIL is older than that, going back to early Kabbalistic writings, but it has clung to his name as a result of the plays of Marlowe (*Dr Faustus*) and Goethe (*Faust*). These were inspired by the book *The History of Doctor Faustus*, published in Germany in 1587. The essence of the story is that Faust makes a bargain with the Devil, under the name of MEPHISTOPHELES, for twenty-four years of life during which he will experience every form of pleasure and gain every kind of knowledge. In exchange, the Devil may have his soul, and in the end the Devil must come to claim his due.

FENG-SHUI

The ancient Chinese occult study of the hidden currents and forces that cover the surface of the earth. Feng-shui in Chinese means 'wind' and 'water'. The direction and spiritual qualities of these forces are of paramount importance in determining the suitability of locations for living, burial and religious centres. Those who practise the discipline of Feng-shui have an intimate knowledge of the workings of the magnetic *Kung-lei* ('dragon paths'), which trace out the powerful earth currents and which appear to be the equivalent of the LEY LINES. Feng-shui was first written down in the ninth century by Yang Yun-sung, and other versions followed.

FERN SEED

Once said to be a recipe for gaining invisibility, a prized aim of occultists. Some kinds of fern seed are so tiny as to be almost invisible, and it was believed that plants could pass their own qualities on to those who carried them.

FETISH

An object representing spirits that is used to create a bond between the human and supernatural world. Fetishes are dolls, carved images, stones, or animal teeth, claws or bones. They are often worn on the body to impart their magical powers, such as for protection, luck, love, curing, warding off evil, money, good hunting, gambling, or curses on enemies. The term 'fetish' may derive from the Latin *factitius*, 'made by art', or the Portuguese *feitico*, 'charm' or 'sorcery'.

Other terms associated with fetishes are 'juju' and 'gris-gris', both of which may have derived from a West African term, *grou-grou*, for sacred objects. Early European traders commonly called the grou-grou they encountered *juju*, meaning dolls or playthings. The gris-gris evolved out of the Afri-can-American slave culture in the American South and refers to charm bags filled with magical powders, herbs, spices, roots, bones, stones, feathers, and so on. Today the term is popularly used to refer to an object or idea that receives superstitious or unquestioning trust or reverence. It is also used in psychiatry to refer to the inordinate or pathological fascination a person may have for an inanimate object.

FINDHORN

An experimental spiritual community founded in 1962 and located in northern Scotland, and the site of a garden seemingly endowed with special powers. At its peak in the late 1960s and early 1970s, Findhorn yielded eighteen-kilogram (forty-pound) cabbages and other plants and flowers that sometimes grew to twice their normal size despite the fact that the soil was nothing more than sand and gravel and the bitter climate of the North Sea made for abysmal growing conditions.

Findhorn residents claimed that they received the directions for planting, cultivating and managing their gardens from spirits that inhabit the natural world. The Findhorn experiment has come to be viewed as a demonstration of the power and potential of human beings and the natural world living and working together in harmony.

Peter Caddy and co-worker Dorothy Maclean, who established the first garden on the site, claimed to have established contact with a spirit of the plant kingdom, called a DEVA, said to hold the archetypal pattern for each individual plant species. The devas provided specific information about every aspect of the garden: how far apart to plant seeds, how often to water, and how to remedy problems.

Within a year Findhorn had been transformed, with the gardens overflowing with life. Cabbages were over ten times their usual weight. Broccoli grew so large that the plants were too heavy to lift from the ground. As word of the garden spread, it became a model community for proponents of the NEW AGE movement. By the early 1970s, more than three hundred people lived, worked and studied in Findhorn. Residents viewed themselves as the vanguard of a new society based on the principles of cooperation between people and the kingdom of nature. By the 1980s the plants, fruits and vegetables had returned to normal sizes, and none of the present gardeners claims direct contact with the natural world. Nevertheless, newer members of the community preserve the original spirit and ideas of the founders. Findhorn has a democratic government, a garden school, and a company to help small businesses within the community.

FISHER KING
In the legend of the HOLY GRAIL, the Fisher or Fisherman King, uncle of the Round Table knight Sir Percival, was the lord of the Castle of the Holy Grail.

FIVE ELEMENTS
In Chinese divination, these elements or forces are seen to underlie the human presence in the landscape. They are Wood – related to Spring, sunrise, East, the colour green, and tall, slender shapes; Fire – related to Summer, mid-day, South, the colour red and triangular shapes; Earth – related to no season or compass point, but to flat shapes and the colour ochre; Metal – related to Autumn, the West, the colour white, and round shapes; and Water – related to Winter, night, the colour black, and to all that is transient and irregular.

FORTEAN PHENOMENA
Any paranormal or strange phenomenon that appears to defy natural explanation, such as rains of frogs, fish, stones, dead birds, flesh and snakes; mystifying religious experiences, such as STIGMATA; floating balls of light in the night sky; spontaneous human combustion; UFOs; POLTERGEIST activity; and monstrous creatures.

Fortean phenomena are named after Charles Fort (1874–1932), an American journalist. After an inheritance enabled him to quit work as a journalist in his early forties, Fort devoted the rest of his life to collecting and cataloguing thousands of odd phenomena that had no explanation, which he found by poring through scientific and popular journals in the British Museum and New York Public Library.

Fort never attempted to explain these phenomena but used these examples to point out the limitations of scientific knowledge and the danger of dogmatic acceptance of natural laws, which the phenomena seemed to contravene. Fort compiled his research into four books: The *Book of the Damned* (1919); *New Lands* (1923); *Lo!* (1931); and *Wild Talents* (1932). In *The Book of the Damned*, which lists over one thousand such incidents, Fort challenged the scientific method of accepting a phenomenon as genuine only if it could be proved. To Fort the fact that a phenomenon had occurred and been reported was proof enough; the reason why was less important.

To demonstrate the folly of scientists who were convinced that there must be an explanation for every event – for example, black rains falling on Scotland between 1863 and 1866 were said by scientists to be the result of eruptions of Mount Vesuvius – Fort advanced his own catch-all theory. He invented the Super-Sargasso Sea, a place above the Earth that contained a collection of matter drawn from the ground below. It was from the Super-Sargasso Sea that the frogs, cannonballs, stones and countless other objects simply fall to the earth. Fort's studies of the inexplicable have continued since his death, research being pursued on a scholarly basis by enthusiasts.

Of major interest to modern Forteans are UFOs and related phenomena. Long before the term 'UFO' was conceived, Fort uncovered reports of sky oddities dating back to 1779. Modern investigations focus on missing time, close encounters and a phenomenon known as the MEN IN BLACK, mysterious people dressed in dark clothing who sometimes purport to be government or United States Air Force representatives, and intimidate UFO witnesses and confiscate UFO photographs taken by private citizens. Two other phenomena, possibly related to UFOs, are the 'mystery helicopters', black helicopters reported all over the world since 1938, years before the helicopter was invented; and 'Mothman', a grey man-sized and man-shaped creature with red eyes, a bill and wings three metres (ten feet) in span. More than one hundred reports of Mothman were made in 1966 and 1967 in an Ohio River valley area; a black Mothman-type creature was reported performing aerial stunts over New York and New Jersey in 1887 and 1880. Forteans also investigate reported sightings of the sasquatch, or Big Foot, the Loch Ness Monster, the Yeti, or Abominable Snowman, and other creatures.

FORTUNE-TELLING
A low-level form of prediction practised at fairs by 'gypsies', using PALMISTRY, card-reading and crystal gazing primarily. It is not a term used by more serious practitioners.

FREEMASONRY
The secret and fraternal organisations believed to have evolved from the medieval guilds of the stonemasons. Membership is open to men only, requires no allegiance to a single faith or religion, although belief in God is necessary, and aims to enable members to meet in harmony, to promote friendship and to be charitable. The orders provide a network for business, professional and social success and advancement. The basic unit of Freemasonry is the lodge, which exists under a charter issued by a grand lodge exercising administrative powers. The lodges are linked together infor-

mally by a system of mutual recognition between lodges that meet the Masonic requirements. The lodge confers three degrees: Entered Apprentice, Fellow Craft, and Master Mason. Additional degrees are conferred by two groups of advanced freemasonry: the York Rite, which awards twelve degrees, and the Scottish Rite, which awards thirty higher degrees.

Many legendary theories exist concerning the origin of Freemasonry, but it is generally linked to the development of medieval craft guilds of stonemasons. Small numbers of skilled stonemasons would travel between towns to build churches and cathedrals commissioned by the clergy. To protect their knowledge they organised themselves into guilds, complete with passwords, rules of procedure, payment and religious devotion.

How the membership of the guilds changed to clubs or lodges attracting largely unskilled, honorary membership is unclear, but Freemasonry's present organisational form began on 24 June 1717, when a grand lodge was formed in London. Since that time lodges have spread all over the world with local grand lodges formed whenever enough lodges exist in an area.

At various times and places freemasonry has met religious and political opposition. Religious opponents, especially the Roman Catholic and Eastern Orthodox churches, have traditionally claimed that Freemasonry is a religion and is a secret organisation. A papal ban on Roman Catholic membership in Masonic lodges was rescinded in 1983. Freemasons hold that the organisation is religious but not a religion, and that it is not a secret organisation since it works openly in the community. Freemasonry has always been suppressed in totalitarian states.

Interest from the outside has always centred on the alleged initiation rites and on the supposed esoteric knowledge conferred on those who attain to the higher degrees of the 'craft'.

There are approximately 4.8 million Freemasons in regular lodges scattered around the world. Many notable men in history have been Freemasons, including Wolfgang Amadeus Mozart, Christopher Wren, Benjamin Franklin, Henry Ford, Rudyard Kipling, Winston Churchill, George Washington and various other American presidents.

FRIAR BUNGAY
A fourteenth-century magician and necromancer, said to have aided Edward IV at the Battle of Barnet by raising mists and vapours.

FRITH
A form of augury (pronounced free) known in the west of Scotland, practised by those endowed with SECOND SIGHT. The seer would fast before the first Monday of the quarter, then stand barefoot, bare-headed and blind-folded on the doorstep at sunrise. Placing a hand on each doorpost, and uttering a short invocation, the seer would remove the blindfold, and make a prediction based on the first thing he or she saw.

FUTHARC
The first six letters of the RUNIC alphabet (*th* is a single letter in the old Germanic languages), which were endowed with a magic significance. Whilst runic writing was sometimes used for ordinary communication, its most frequent use was for ceremonial purposes.

G

GALGAL

A modern form of divination based on a combination of methods found in the KABBALAH: the Tree of Life and the Hebrew alphabet.

GAMALEI

Certain natural stones or gems, which, because of some powerful astrological influence, were said by medieval occultists to be magically efficacious. Artificial gamalei are those engraved with astrological, HERMETIC or magical symbols, for use as TALISMANS. *See also* BIRTH STONES.

GANZFELD STIMULATION

An experimental technique used in PARAPSYCHOLOGY since the 1970s to create an environment of sensory deprivation to stimulate the receptivity of ESP. *Ganzfeld* means 'whole field' in German and refers to the blank field of vision that confronts a test subject. In a ganzfeld test a receiver attempts to perceive thoughts and impressions transmitted by a sender.

The receiver is placed in a soundproof room, wears eye cups to remove visual distractions (the eyes remain open throughout the procedure) and earphones to mask sounds. The sender is seated in a similar soundproof room and given an image to focus on and transmit, selected at random by a computer. At the end of the session, the receiver is shown a selection of images and asked to pick the target. The removal of extraneous sensory data creates a sense of disorientation in the receiver, and the subject may have periods of 'blank out' similar to a hypnotic or meditative state. According to the research results, it is during these periods that subjects are most receptive, with success rates of up to 50 per cent, compared to the expected chance rate of 5 per cent.

GELLER, URI (b. 1946)

An Israeli psychic renowned for his abilities to bend metal objects by stroking or looking at them, and to stop watches or make them run faster. Such feats of PSYCHOKINESIS (PK) are called by some the 'Geller effect'. During the peak of his public career in the 1970s, Geller worked full-time as a professional performer who demonstrated his metal-bending and mind-reading abilities for television audiences worldwide. By the end of the decade, he was devoting most of his time to private consulting with occasional public appearances. Despite his successful feats, most parapsychologists have not taken him seriously, perhaps because of his entertainment career.

Geller claims he discovered his psychic powers when he was five years old, following an incident involving his mother's sewing machine. He saw a tiny blue spark coming from the machine, and when he tried to touch it, he received a violent shock and was knocked off his feet. He says that his new powers manifested immediately, including an ability to read his mother's mind. A year later he found he could make the hands speed up on a watch his father had given to him. Shortly afterwards the spoon bending began. He became a full-time performer in 1969. Geller was tested in 1972 at the Stanford Research Institute (SRI) in California. He gave impressive demonstrations of ESP, but tests to prove his metal-bending abilities were inconclusive. As a professional performer, Geller was in constant demand throughout the 1970s. He travelled the world, making frequent television and radio appearances. Following most of these, broadcasters were flooded by calls from viewers and listeners who reported that their silverware had been bent or watches and clocks had begun working improperly.

Geller's high profile made him an enticing target for debunkers, who attempted to demonstrate how they could perform the same metal-bending feats using stage magic. In the late 1970s, Geller retired from the public limelight, save for occasional appearances, and began private consulting work, including DOWSING for minerals and oil.

GEMATRIA

A Kabbalistic system (*see* KABBALA) for discovering the hidden meaning of letters, words and sentences, using numbers and letters of the alphabet. The system is based on the fact that the letters of the Hebrew alphabet have been accorded numerical equivalents, in which the numerical value of letters in words are added together to give specific values. Words of similar numerical values are regarded as having correspondences or analogies in accordance with a complex mystical system, which is used to determine the precise meaning and significance of the scriptures, or of a sacred building or holy object.

GEMINI

The third sign of the ZODIAC.

dates: 22 May to 21 June.

origin and glyph: two children, from Castor and Pollux of Classical mythology, which are bright stars.

ruling planet and groupings: Mercury; masculine, mutable and air.

typical traits: these include such characteristics as liveliness, versatility and intelligence, but these are tempered to some degree by a nervous energy and a certain inconsistency at times. They are logical, ordered and very quick of mind, seeking variety in their lives, both at home and in their work. They tend to be good communicators but at times let their desire to communicate dominate all else. They can take in information very quickly if they are concentrating enough, but run the risk of knowing a little about a lot rather than grasping one topic in great depth. This is not necessarily a bad thing, of course.

family: the Geminian curiosity and versatility render relationships a little more prone than most to disruption or diversion. However, partnerships can last, particularly if the husband/wife finds an interesting companion with whom he or she can interact intellectually. Gemini women often marry men who can deal with domestic chores, as such women have no love of housework.

As parents, they can be lively and creative but sometimes over-critical. It is not uncommon for Geminians to make poor parents because they can be too impatient, too heavily involved in their own careers and over-competitive, seeking reflected glory in their children's achievements.

Gemini children are likely to talk and walk relatively early, and it will be necessary to keep them well occupied. It is often advisable to encourage them to finish anything they have started, to ensure numerous tasks are not left in various stages of completion. Because Geminians can also be quite cunning, and although they may be very able at school, they can often put their own thoughts before hard facts.

business: Geminians are very good when dealing with money and can, therefore, be admirably suited to banking or accountancy. As might be expected, the ability to communicate and the lively personality mean they may also fit well into employment in some aspect of the media or advertising. The pitfalls inevitably are that attention to detail may be lacking and that there must be variety. Conversely, they handle pressure well and are good at handling several tasks at once.

wider aspects: change and variety remain of paramount importance, whether in leisure pursuits or retirement. Individualism will dominate over group activities, which may become routine.

associations: *colour* – yellow, although most are liked; *flowers* – lavender, lily of the valley; *gemstone* – agate; *trees* – any tree producing nuts; *food* – salads and fruit, fish.

GENII

In the GNOSTIC hierarchies, the genii are the ranks of ANGELS. In Arabic lore the genii are the jinx (*see* GENIUS).

GENIUS

In Assyro-Babylonian demonology the *genii* or *jinn* were DE-MONS who participated closely in the everyday life of human beings, although they themselves were invisible and super-human. Good *jinn* were called *shedu* or *lamassu* and would act as guardians (although they required propitiatory rites). Evil *jinn*, called *edimmu*, were said to be the souls of the dead who had not been properly buried.

GEOMANCY *see* APPARITION.

GHOST *see* APPARITION.

GHOUL

A word said to come from the Arabian *ghul* ('to seize') and used to denote an evil spirit, reputed to haunt graveyards and to feed on corpses.

GIFT OF TONGUES *see* GLOSSOLALIA.

GLASTONBURY

Located in the West Country, on the plains of Somerset Levels, not far from the Bristol Channel, Glastonbury is one of the oldest sacred sites in England. Its history is intertwined with the HOLY GRAIL and Arthurian legends. The site includes an abbey, town and Glastonbury Tor, a terraced volcanic rock topped with the remains of an old church tower. The area is believed to rest at the intersection of powerful LEY LINES of earth energy. Its mystical lore draws numerous pilgrims and visitors from around the world. Archaeological evidence indicates the area was inhabited from the third or fourth century BC; the site may have been sacred to the Druids. The town was nearly on an island, surrounded by marshlands, until the sixteenth century, suggesting it may have been associated with the mysterious island of Avalon in Arthurian lore.

Various legends are associated with the Tor. One holds that King Arthur once had a stronghold atop the Tor, which provided entrance to Annwn, the Underworld. Monks built a church there during the Middle Ages; it was destroyed in an earthquake. The present remains are of a later church. According to another legend, Chalice Well, located at the base of the Tor, is said to have been built by the Druids. Its reddish, mineral-laden waters are reputed to have magical powers. Another legend has it that Joseph of Arimathea, the great-uncle of Jesus, brought the boy Jesus on a trip to Glastonbury and later built Britain's first above-ground Christian church below the Tor. He threw the chalice used by Jesus at the Last Supper into the Chalice Well.

The abbey was founded in the fifth century. St Patrick, the legendary founder, is said to have lived and died there and was buried there. Various churches were built at the site over the centuries. The last, dating from the thirteenth or fourteenth century, was destroyed under Henry VIII, who closed down all the abbeys and monasteries in 1539 after his split with the Catholic church. In the ruins the famous Glastonbury Thorn blooms every year, said to be the staff of Joseph of Arimathea, which took root when he leaned upon it. Arthur and Guinevere are buried in secret graves in the abbey grounds, according to legend. In 1190 monks found remains of a man and the inscription, 'Here lies the renowned Arthur in the Isle of Avalon'. The bones were reburied in a black marble tomb in 1278, which was destroyed in the dissolution of the abbey in 1539.

The ruins of Glastonbury were purchased by the Church of England in 1907 for excavation under the direction of Frederick Bligh Bond. Bond was extraordinarily successful in locating unknown chapels and parts of the abbey, and concluded that the abbey's construction had involved sacred geometry known by the builders of the Egyptian pyramids and passed down through the stonemasons. Bond claimed to have received helpful information from the spirits of monks who had lived there and who communicated to him through AUTOMATIC WRITING (*see* GLASTONBURY SCRIPTS, PSYCHIC ARCHAEOLOGY). Bond's belief that Glastonbury is connected to Stonehenge and Avebury by leys has been upheld by modern ley investigators; the entire theory of leys, however, remains controversial.

In 1929 it was discovered that natural formations in the Glastonbury area recreate the twelve signs of the ZODIAC (*see* GLASTONBURY ZODIAC). The origins of the patterns are unknown. Glastonbury is the site of Christian pilgrimages and seasonal rituals practised by ritual magicians, witches, and pagans, and of various occult and spiritual festivals. Bright and fiery lights have been seen hovering over the Tor. They may be some form of unexplained natural energy. UFO watchers believe that they are connected with extraterrestrial spacecraft.

GLASTONBURY SCRIPTS

A general name given to a series of manuscripts produced through AUTOMATIC WRITING between 1907 and 1912, under the guidance of the architect Frederick Bligh Bond, with specific regard to the restoration of Glastonbury Abbey. Many details concerning the dissolution of the monastery, seemingly known only to the spirit world, were revealed to Bond and later verified by him (*see* PSYCHIC ARCHAEOLOGY). In the last series of scripts appeared accurate prophecies relating to the coming and ending of World War I.

GLASTONBURY ZODIAC

The name given to a supposed earth ZODIAC, contained within a fifteen-kilometre (ten-mile) wide circle, with Butleigh (Somerset) at the centre and Glastonbury Tor to north-northwest of the circle. The figures were originally traced out by Katherine Maltwood, a sculptor and illustrator (after whom the zodiac is sometimes named) in 1929. In the sixteenth century Dr John DEE, astrologer to Queen Elizabeth I, had mentioned the existence of a zodiac in or around Glastonbury, but his descriptions are vague and there is no evidence that this so-called Dee Zodiac corresponds to the Glastonbury zodiac. The images (which do not in every case correspond to either zodiacal or constellational images) are supposed to be traced out in landscape contours, roads, earthworks, rivers, pools and other natural formations.

GLOSSOLALIA

A Christian religious phenomenon in which the believer, in an ecstatic state, speaks in a foreign language or utters unintelligible sounds that are taken to contain a divine message. Many Christians believe the genuine gift of tongues to have been confined to earliest Christianity and first came to the apostles at Pentecost, or the celebration seven weeks after Passover. Classic Pentecostal Christians see speaking in tongues as a definite sign of baptism by the Holy Spirit. Other groups that advocate glossolalia are the Shakers, Quakers and Latter-day Saints, or Mormons. Early Methodists spoke in tongues, as did some Presbyterians during the 1830s.

During the Shakers' wave of spiritual manifestations (1837–47), worshippers composed hymns and prayers in tongues delivered by the spirits. Since these languages were unintelligible to mortals, the songs were learned phonetically. Modern charismatics, such as the Pentacostalists and charismatics, maintain that the worshipper may or may not speak in tongues following the conversion experience. Like the gifts of healing, wisdom, PROPHECY, miracles and spirit DIVINATION, the ability to speak in tongues is not given to everyone. Many psychologists explain the phenomenon as a hypnotic trance that results from religious excitement.

GLYPH

In astrology, a particular graphical representation allocated to each sign of the zodiac and to the planets, which relates to an animal or something similar. These symbols are used, with others, in constructing an astrological chart.

Sign	Representation	Name
Aries	the ram's horns	The Ram
Taurus	the bull's head	The Bull
Gemini	two children	The Twins
Cancer	breasts	The Crab
Leo	the heart, or the lion's tail	The Lion
Virgo	the female genitalia	The Virgin
Libra	a pair of scales	The Balance
Scorpio	the male genitalia	The Scorpion

Sagittarius	the Centaur's arrow	The Archer
Capricorn	a goat's head and fish's tail	The Goat
Aquarius	waves of water or air	The Water-bearer
Pisces	two fish	The Fishes

These glyphs of the planet are all made up of essentially the same elements, the cross, half-circle and circle, all in different combinations. These pictorial representations are linked with the very early days of human beings, when communication was achieved using such graphical methods. As such, these elements each have a particular significance:

—the circle represents eternity, something without end, the spirit;

—a dot inside a circle represents the spirit or power beginning to come out;

—the cross represents the material world;

—and the semicircle stands for the soul.

In some civilisations, the signs were attributed to parts of the body. The likeliest race to have adopted this were the Greeks, who also linked the signs to various plants.

GNOMES

A class of NATURE SPIRITS linked with the earth. They have many different names in popular lore and are said to be visible to clairvoyants as dwarfish humans who live in caves and the mountains.

GNOSTICS AND GNOSTICISM

Gnosticism, derived from a Greek word *gnosis* meaning 'knowledge', is applied to a philosophical and religious movement that influenced the Mediterranean world from the first century BC to the third century AD. It expressed itself in a variety of pagan, Jewish and Christian forms. Its name is derived from the fact that it promised salvation through a secret knowledge or understanding of reality possessed by its devotees. Previously known mostly from the writings of its Christian opponents, Gnosticism can now be studied in a collection of original documents found near the Egyptian town of Nag Hammadi in 1945 (also called the Dead Sea Scrolls).

Despite the complex diversity of Gnostic groups and their teachings, the basic doctrines of Gnosticism formed an identifiable pattern of belief and practice. A pervasive dualism underlay much of Gnostic thought. Good and evil, light and darkness, truth and falsehood, spirit and matter were opposed to one another in human experience as being and nonbeing. The created universe and human experience were characterised by a radical disjunction between the spiritual, which was real, and the physical, which was illusory. This disjunction resulted from a cosmic tragedy, described in a variety of ways by Gnostic mythology, as a consequence of which sparks of deity became entrapped in the physical world. These could be freed only by saving knowledge that was revealed to a spiritual elite by a transcendent messenger from the spirit world, variously identified as Seth (one of the sons of Adam), Jesus, or some other figure. Renunciation of physical desires and strict asceticism, combined with mystical rites of initiation and purification, were thought to liberate the immortal souls of believers from the prison of physical existence. Reunion with divine reality was accomplished after a journey of the soul through intricate systems of hostile powers.

Associated in legend with Simon Magus, a Samaritan sorcerer mentioned in the Bible in Acts 8:9–24, gnosticism probably originated in the Near East as a synthesis of Eastern and Greek ideas before the advent of Christianity. It reached the height of its influence as a Christian sect in the middle of the second century AD, when it was represented by the Egyptian teachers Basilides and Valentinus. As Christian orthodoxy was defined in the period that followed, Gnosticism began to decline and gradually was pushed to the periphery of the Christian world or driven underground by the persecution of church leaders. Some Gnostic tendencies found their way into later Christian monasticism, while others survived among the Mandaeans and adherents of Manichaeism.

Interest in the Gnostics was revived in the twentieth century with the discovery of Gnostic manuscripts, previously thought to be lost, in Turkestan between 1902 and 1914 and near Nag Hammadi in upper Egypt in 1945 and 1946 and in 1948. The latter are usually called the Dead Sea Scrolls and have provided the basis for new interpretations of Gnostic beliefs and influence. Another major factor in the reexamination of Gnosticism is the work of the Swiss psychiatrist Carl Gustav JUNG. Between 1912 and 1926, Jung delved into a study of Gnosticism and early Christianity. He found in Gnosticism an early, prototypical depth psychology. He believed that Christianity, and as a result Western culture, had suffered because of the repression of Gnostic concepts. In looking for ways to reintroduce Gnostic ideas to modern culture, Jung found them in alchemy. The first codex of the Nag Hammadi library found in 1945 was purchased and given to Jung on his eightieth birthday. It is called the Codex Jung.

GOETIC
Pertaining to that magic involving the evocation and binding of evil spirits to the service of humans.

GOG AND MAGOG
Identified in the Book of Revelation as the future enemies of the kingdom of God, and identified generally with the forces of darkness and Antichrist.

GRAIL, HOLY *see* HOLY GRAIL.

GRAND GRIMOIRE
The name given to a collection of invocations, spells and elementary magic, supposedly from the pen of King Solomon but almost certainly no older than the sixteenth century.

GREY MAN
A phenomenon seen by mountain climbers, especially on certain mountains, like Ben Macdhui in Scotland, and usually associated with misty conditions. A grey looming figure appears to be accompanying the climbers. The probable explanation is a visual trick of mist and light. Polar explorers have reported a similar experience, not visual in origin, however, in which a small group of two or three trudging walkers felt the presence of an extra member walking with them.

GRIMOIRES
A general name given to a variety of texts setting out the names of demons, along with instructions for raising them to do the bidding of the magician or 'operator'. The *Grimorium Serum* lists seventeen of the names and characters of such spirits, each with its own particular field of interest: for example,

Glauneck, who has power over riches and hidden treasures; Bechard, who has power over winds and tempests, and so on.

The Lesser Key of Solomon gives the names and symbols for seventy-two spirits. For example, Agares is a duke who rides a crocodile and carries a goshawk on his wrist; his main function is to stop runaways, teach languages, destroy spiritual and temporal dignities, and to cause earthquakes. Behemoth is a demon concerned with the pleasures of the belly. Sytry is a great prince with a leopard's head; his function is to procure sex or love for the magician. Buns is a powerful duke with the heads of dog, griffin and man; his function is to change the place of burials and to answer all questions put to him by the magician. Astaroth is a powerful duke, appearing in the guise of an angel or a dragon, with a viper in his right hand. The magician must not permit him to approach because of the stench of his breath, and must protect himself with a special magical ring. Astaroth will answer truthfully about all manner of past, present and future questions. Similar grimoires are the GRAND GRIMOIRE, the HEPTAMERON, the Enchiridium, the *Grimorium Verum*, the *Grimoire of Honorius* and the *Key of Solomon*.

GROUPINGS

In astrology, the twelve signs of the Zodiac are subdivided into a number of groups, the members of each group sharing certain characteristics that provide additional information rather than primary details. The first grouping is the triplicities, or ELEMENTS. Aries, Leo and Sagittarius are the Fire triplicity; the Earth triplicity is Taurus, Virgo and Capricorn. Gemini, Libra and Aquarius form the Air triplicity. The Water triplicity contains Cancer, Scorpio and Pisces.

The quadruplicities, or qualities, are cardinal (Aries, Libra, Cancer and Capricorn), fixed (Taurus, Scorpio, Leo and Aquarius) and mutable (Germini, Sagittarius, Virgo and Pisces). Another grouping is into positive and negative, or masculine and feminine, and equates to being extrovert (positive) on the one hand or introvert on the other.

GURDJIEFF, GEORGE IVANOVICH (1872?–1949)

Russian-born spiritual leader and founder of a movement based on doctrines of enlightenment through meditation and heightened self-awareness that attracted many prominent followers in Europe and the United States. He is regarded by some as the greatest mystical teacher of all time, and by others as a fraud. Although he was aware of THEOSOPHY and other contemporary occult-spiritual philosophies, Gurdjieff decided to establish his own. He postulated that people are no more than machines controlled by external forces beyond their control, a condition analogous to being asleep. To wake up, various techniques must be used to penetrate the normal state of unconsciousness to access the true consciousness within. These Gurdjieffian techniques include specially adapted forms of HYPNOTISM, total obedience to a teacher who has achieved enlightenment (a Man Who Knows), constant self-observation, hard physical labour, demeaning tasks, intense emotionalism, exercise and dance routines.

The aim of the 'system' was to 'shock' the subject into a state of new self-awareness, allowing him or her to transcend mechanical existence and commune harmoniously with the true soul. Gurdjieff established his Institute for the Harmonious Development of Man at Fontainebleau, France, where he settled in 1922. His disciples included the architect Frank

Lloyd Wright, the painter Georgia O'Keeffe, the writer Katherine Mansfield, and the journalist P. D. Ouspensky, whose books helped to popularise Gurdjieff's teachings.

GWYN AP NUDD
A figure from Welsh mythology, the lord of Annwn, land of the dead. He is also linked with 'Gwyn', king of the fairies, said to hold court on the summit of GLASTONBURY TOR.

GYROMANCY
Said to be a method of divination in which the diviner walks around a circle of letters until he or she is too giddy to continue; the letters against which he stumbles are supposed to spell out a prophetic message.

HALLOWE'EN

All Hallows Eve, 31 October, the day before All Saints' Day and traditionally the time when evil spirits were free to roam abroad. It marked the end of the year in the ancient Celtic calendar, and its significance goes back far before Christianity. Its modern 'trick or treat' aspect goes back to a time when children dressed up, perhaps to propitiate the roving spirits or make them believe that the houses had already been visited.

HARUSPEX

The Latin name for a diviner, originally derived from the Etruscan method of DIVINATION, which involved the foretelling of future events from an examination of the entrails of slaughtered animals. The word may have been derived from the Sanskrit root *hira* ('entrails'). A synonymous term is EXTISPICY.

HAUNTING

Mysterious happenings attributed to the presence of ghosts or spirits. Phenomena include apparitions, noises, smells, tactile sensations, extremes in temperature, movement of objects, and the like. Despite much scientific inquiry since the late nineteenth century, very little is known about the nature of hauntings and why they happen. The term 'haunt' is derived from the same root as 'home' and refers to the occupation of homes by the spirits of deceased people and animals who lived there. Other haunted sites seem to be places merely frequented or liked by the deceased, or places where violent death has occurred.

Most hauntings have no clear reason or purpose. Some are continual and others are active only on certain dates that correspond to the deaths or major events in the lives of the deceased. Some hauntings are brief, lasting only a few weeks, months or years, while others continue for centuries. Haunted places often are pervaded by an oppressive atmosphere. Not everyone who goes to a haunted place experiences paranormal phenomena. The theory is that only individuals with certain psychic attunements or emotional states are receptive. Few hauntings involve seeing apparitions. In those that do, a GHOST may be seen by a single individual or collectively by several people present at the same time.

Thousands of hauntings have been investigated by psychical researchers and parapsychologists over the last hundred years or so. Numerous theories have been advanced, all inconclusive. Some early psychic researchers thought that ghosts were meaningless fragments of energy left behind in death. Others have theorised that hauntings are a form of psychometry, vibrations of events and emotions imbued into a house, site or object. One popular spiritualist theory holds that hauntings occur when the spirit of the dead person or animal is trapped on the earth plane for various reasons, doesn't know it is dead or is reluctant to leave. Gentle exorcisms will send the spirit on to the afterworld (*see* SPIRITUALISM).

Researchers employ three basic techniques to investigate a haunting. These are description, experimentation and detection. Description involves taking eyewitness accounts. Experimentation involves bringing a psychic to the site to corroborate the eyewitness accounts or provide new information. Detection involves the observation or recording of phenomena using a ghost-hunter's kit, including camcorders, infrared cameras and tape recorders, as well as heat sensors and Geiger counters to measure changes in the atmosphere. Such methods are at best imprecise and interpretation of results is often subjective. Critics say ghost investigation is imprecise and not a true science because it is heavily reliant upon eyewitness testimony. *See* APPARITION, POLTERGEIST.

HECATE
Originally one of the giant Titans of Greek mythology who were subdued by Zeus. She was the only one to retain her powers, to become the triple-headed demon goddess regarded by the ancient Greeks as the queen of darkness, death, sexual perversity and, most of all, witchcraft.

HELL-FIRE CLUB
This society was founded by the profligate Sir Francis Dashwood (1708–81), at his country house at Medmenham, near Henley on Thames, England. The real name was The Knights of St Francis of Wycombe, but the locals referred to

them as the Mad Monks. Their doings were more in the way of sexual orgies and drinking bouts but with an occult tinge to increase the sense of danger and of outrage to civilised society.

HEPTAMERON
The title of a book dealing with the invocation of spirits in the style of the GRIMOIRES, with a second part touching upon elementary magical practices, such as the secrets of hidden things, love procuration and the conveyance of evil thoughts. The first part of the text is supposed to be by the Italian magician-astrologer Peter of Abano, although it was certainly not written before the fourteenth century.

HERBA SACRA
From Latin, 'sacred weed', a name for the herb *Verbena*, vervain, which was once believed to have magical powers to avert sorcery and to cure the bite of rabid animals as well as the plague.

HERMANN PROPHECIES
A series of prophecies (first printed around 1722) supposedly by a monk called Hermann. These consisted of a hundred sentences of a predictive nature and gained much popularity in France, especially during World War I, as they prophesied the eventual downfall of Germany and the Hohenzollern Empire and the redistribution of German lands.

HERMES
The Greek name for the god Mercury. Alchemists (*see* ALCHEMY) usually referred to quicksilver as Hermes rather than Mercury.

HERMES TRISMEGISTUS

The name means 'thrice-greatest Hermes'. It was given by Neo-Platonic philosophers to the supposed founder of AL-CHEMY, the ancient Egyptian god THOTH. *See also* HERMETICA.

HERMETICA

Mystical wisdom that, together with the KABBALAH, formed the foundation of Western occultism. The term is derived from the surviving fragments of a multi-volume work known as the *Corpus Hermeticum*, or *Hermetica*. This mystical philosophical work was allegedly written by Hermes Trismegistus ('Thrice-Greatest'), a mythical composite of the Egyptian god THOTH and the Greek god Hermes. The fragments present a synthesis of Kabbalistic, Neo-Platonic and Christian mystical and spiritual traditions. According to legend, the Hermetic books were written on papyrus and stored in one of the great libraries in Alexandria. Most were lost when the library was burned. Surviving fragments supposedly were buried in a secret desert location known only to select initiates.

Controversy over the age and authorship of the *Hermetica* has existed since at least the Renaissance. Isaac Casaubon (1559–1614), French classical scholar and theologian, claimed that the works were not of Egyptian origin but were written by early Christians or semi-Christians. Casaubon's exegesis helped to bring about a decline in the Renaissance interest in magic. In all likelihood, the Hermetic works were written much later than Casaubon believed, by multiple anonymous authors who used the pseudonym 'Hermes Trismegistus'.

HERNE THE HUNTER

In the English version of the common European legend of the 'wild huntsman', his name is Herne or Hern. A spectral figure who rides through the forest with a ghost-pack of hounds, he strikes terror into the mortals who catch sight of him.

HEXAGRAM

In the Chinese divinatory system of the I CHING, a name given to a six-line figure made from two trigrams (a triple combination of Yin and Yang lines). Within this figure the Chinese diviner will trace a second pair of trigrams, called the nuclear trigrams. The hexagram, its basic and nuclear trigrams, and the associations drawn between these three elements are combined by the diviner to give responses to questions. Sometimes a consultation of the classical text of the *I Ching* is also resorted to.

HOLY GRAIL

The Holy Grail, a symbolic TALISMAN around which numerous medieval legends and poems revolve, probably originated in Celtic pagan tradition as the cup of plenty and regeneration, symbol of the Great Mother. In the Christian era, the Grail became associated with the cup used at the Last Supper in which Joseph of Arimathea collected blood from Christ's wounds. Joseph was said to have brought the grail to GLASTONBURY. The Grail was sought by the knights of King Arthur in several medieval romances, the earliest of which was the late-twelfth-century *Perceval* by Chrétien de Troyes. The quest for the Grail, which can be found only by a hero free from sin, is treated at length in the *Morte d'Arthur* (*c*.1469) of Sir Thomas Malory and in Wolfram von Eschenbach's epic, *Parzifal* (*c*. 1210), which inspired the German composer Richard Wagner's opera *Parsifal* (1877–82). The other objects associated with the Holy Grail are the Sword, the Dish and the Spear. Much Grail material has been dragged into the Germanic-Nordic mythology and pseudo-Occultism created by the National Socialist (Nazi) movement in Germany, allegedly by way of the TEUTONIC KNIGHTS. *See also* MERLIN.

HOME, DANIEL DUNGLAS (1833–86)

A Scottish spiritualist medium who was brought up in the United States. He was successful in establishing with many people that he was genuine and was never exposed as a fraud, although the poet Robert Browning remained sceptical and made Home the subject of his poem 'Mr Sludge, the Medium' (1864). *See also* ELONGATION; LEVITATION.

HOODOO SEA *see* BERMUDA TRIANGLE.

HORARY ASTROLOGY

The astrological art of interpreting specific questions in terms of a chart erected for the moment when the question is formulated (the word 'horary' meaning 'relating to the hours').

HOROSCOPE

An important element in astrology which interprets the character and destiny of a person (and occasionally a larger group) according to the position of the planets, usually at the time of the person's birth. A horoscope is cast on the basis of information given by the person, and it is then interpreted according to systematic principles. The horoscope takes into account two main considerations: the circle of the twelve signs of the ZODIAC (Aries, Taurus, Gemini, Cancer, Leo, Virgo, Libra, Scorpio, Sagittarius, Capricorn, Aquarius, Pisces) as they are crossed by the Sun, Moon and planets at different periods; and a circle of twelve 'houses' around which the circle of the zodiac turns. Casting a horoscope is a complicated procedure that depends upon getting data and times right. Relevant factors are the position of Sun, Moon, planets and signs of the zodiac; the ASPECTS of Sun, Moon and planets in relation to each other; and the position of Sun, Moon, planets and signs of the zodiac against the circle of twelve HOUSES. Certain planets are thought to be allied with certain activities and human propensities (for example, Venus with love); the twelve houses are thought to be connected with certain areas of life, for example, the second house with money; and the aspects are thought to be associated with helpful or unhelpful situations and possibilities. Horoscopes remain important in the East and are growing in popular significance in the West despite scientific scepticism.

HOSPITALLERS, KNIGHTS

Founded in 1070 as part of the Crusading movement, the Knights Hospitallers (Knights of St John of Jerusalem) were a brotherhood who maintained the lodging for pilgrims at Jerusalem while it was not occupied by the Moors and also ran a hospital. They were also at later dates granted the islands of Rhodes and then Malta. As a brotherhood, they had their rites and secrets, many of the latter concerned with the methods of eastern medicine they had learned from Arabs and Indians.

HOUSES

In astrology, the traditional HOROSCOPE figure is divided into twelve arcs, which are symbolically presented as being equal either in a spatial system or in a time system. This division is superimposed upon the projected celestial sphere, with the symbolic horizon line (usually) marking the cusps of the first and seventh houses (the east point and west point, respectively). The tenth house cusp marks the symbolic zenith, called the medium coeli, while the fourth house cusp marks the symbolic nadir, called the imum coeli.

HYDROMANCY

A name given to various different methods of predicting the future by means of water. One technique supposedly involved a basin full of water which, at the command of the diviner, is activated by spirits in order to vibrate to a point where it appears to boil and give off meaningful sounds. Methods of disturbing water (by means of suspended rings or by means of pebbles being dropped into the bowl) are also described as legitimate hydromantic techniques, and some diviners are supposed to read from the reflections on the surface or from the colour of water as well as from the movement of water in fountains.

HYPNOSIS

A state or condition in which an individual becomes highly responsive to suggestions and may also exhibit enhanced psychic abilities. The hypnotised person seems to follow instructions in an uncritical, automatic fashion and to attend closely only to those aspects of the environment indicated by the hypnotist. A profoundly responsive subject hears, sees, feels, smells and tastes in accordance with the hypnotist's suggestions, even though they may be in direct contradiction to the actual stimuli impinging upon the subject. Further, memory and awareness of self can be altered by suggestions. All of these effects may be extended posthypnotically into the individual's later waking activity.

The Austrian physician Anton MESMER discovered hypnotism in the 1770s, calling it 'animal magnetism'. As a therapeutic technique, animal magnetism – or mesmerism – spread throughout Europe. It was discovered that subjects felt no pain under surgery and that in some cases side effects of a deep magnetised trance included CLAIRVOYANCE, TELEPATHY, REMOTE VIEWING and eyeless vision. In the 1840s, the Scottish surgeon James Braid, who coined the term 'hypnosis' from the Greek word for sleep, advanced the study of the subject. He developed more precise methods and discovered that a hypnotic trance could be induced by merely staring at a bright light or by suggestion alone.

Subsequent physicians in the nineteenth century elaborated the theory that in a hypnotic trance a patient's will was paralysed and that unconscious mental processes could be observed. This led to the concept, developed by the psychoanalyst Sigmund Freud and others, that through hypnosis a patient's repressed thoughts and desires could be revealed. This concept remained dominant until well into the twentieth century, when alternative theories arose, that hypnosis is nothing more than a deep form of relaxation, or that patients under hypnosis are merely 'role-playing', or that the hypnotic state is only one more level of the human system of cognition. In fact, while much is now known about the physiology of the hypnotic trance, its precise causes are still little understood.

Hypnosis has been shown to be effective in enhancing memory and learning, and in treating various physical and psychological disorders. Hypnosis and relaxation exercises have been integrated into many alternative treatments. Some mediums use self-hypnosis to communicate with spirits during CHANNELLING, and during parapsychological experiments it has been used to enhance the abilities of those psychics who specialise in REMOTE VIEWING.

I CHING

The name of a sacred book, also called *The Book of Changes,* which forms the basis for an ancient Chinese divinatory system. The *I Ching* is one of the central texts of Confucianism and one of the earliest works of Chinese literature. It consists of sixty-four hexagrams, each of which is made up of six divided or undivided lines. A hexagram is decided by the results of tossing three coins three times or by tossing fifty yarrow stalks. The solid lines represent the Yang, or male active energy, the broken lines represent Yin, or female receptive energy. Yin and Yang have other attributes: they can be construed as light and dark or positive and negative. This is not the same opposition as good and evil, but rather that of the Sun and the Moon. The diviner can provide guidance on specific questions by interpreting the figures, but it is also possible to refer to a sequence of texts relating to each of the hexagrams in the text of the *I Ching* itself.

The foundation of the *I Ching* dates back to thousands of

years ago in Chinese history and consists of a main text, possibly originating in the second millennium BC, with additions possibly dating from the first millennium BC and a treatise on the text, the *Ten Wings*, credited to Confucius and written at the end of the first millennium BC. Although rejected by the empiricist scholars of the Qing (Ch'ng) dynasty, the numerological aspects of the work have been re-emphasised by Westerners interested in Eastern mysticism. The work was translated in the nineteenth century by James Legge and Richard Wilhelm. Wilhelm's translation included a forward by the psychoanalyst Carl Jung, who saw the text as a means of accessing the subconscious through meditation upon the symbols.

ILLUMINATI

A term for a group of people who were members of sects or secret societies and believed in 'Illuminism', which is applied to the process of direct spiritual and esoteric enlightenment by means of revelation from a higher source or the inspiration of human reason. It is associated with various occult sects and secret orders, including the ROSICRUCIANS and the FREEMASONS. The most highly organised sect, the Order of Illuminati, was founded in Bavaria in 1776 by Adam Weishaupt, a professor of law. Weishaupt may have created the order because he aspired to join the Masons, which he did in 1777. In 1780 he was joined by Baron von Knigge, a respected and high-level Mason, which enabled him to incorporate Masonic elements into his organisational structure and rites. The Order aimed to spread a new religion based on enlightened reason derived from direct contact with Divine Reason.

Illuminism was also antimonarchial, and its identification with republicanism gained it many members throughout Germany. In 1784 Masonry was denounced to the Bavarian government as politically dangerous, which led to the suppression of all secret orders, including the Masons and Illuminati. The Order of Illuminati included such distinguished figures as the German poet Goethe, CAGLIOSTRO, and Franz Anton MESMER.

ILLUMINISM *see* ILLUMINATI.

INCANTATION

Chants were very much a part of occult practice. With the correct words, they could reach to the spirits of the beyond, either to placate them or to summon them. Their rhythmic and repetitive quality helped to create the right state of mind among those assisting at a ritual, while the lengthy and strange-sounding names and words added to the sense of mystery and awe felt by the participants. The real purpose was to work the magician-chanter up to a state of ecstasy in which she or he might experience revelations, like the SHAMAN with his drum.

Chants could include Kabbalistic (*see* KABBALAH) names like Adonai, Elohim, Sabaoth, or with Egyptian ones like those of Horus, Hathor or Thoth. Incantations could be prolonged. One leading practitioner (Aleister CROWLEY) admitted that on one occasion he incorporated the whole text of the hymn 'From Greenland's Icy Mountains' into an incantation and added that determinedly persisting with an absurdity was in itself a way of achieving the desired mental state.

INCUBUS

In occult lore, a lewd male DEMON or goblin who takes on the illusory appearance of a male human being and seeks sexual intercourse with women, usually while they are asleep. The corresponding female demon who appears to men is the SUC-CUBUS. The term 'incubus' is from the Latin *incubo*, meaning 'burden' or 'weight'. It may have become applied to demonic lovers because it was thought that nightmares involving a feeling of oppressive weight on the chest were the consequence of the act of somnambulant copulation with a fiend.

INDEX

The *Index Librorum Prohibitorum* ('list of forbidden books') and the *Index Expurgatorius* were and are the Catholic Church's lists of books that the faithful should not read. They contained all titles of an occult nature which the compilers had knowledge of, seen as dangerously subversive of true religion, as well as many books that would be considered quite harmless today.

INVOCATION

The summoning of a spirit, whether of a dead person or a DEMON. In preparation for this, the magician was required to fast, to perform ritual cleansing and to wear white (or, alternatively, to wear nothing). The reasons for this were the avoidance of contamination from powerful and perhaps unfriendly spirits, and also to increase the ADEPT's sense of power. Fasting has always been used as an aid to building up psychic energy. In more recent times, some magicians have used an opposite technique, of alcohol, drugs and orgiastic sex, in order to reach a state of mental exaltation. A secluded place was necessary, free from interruption, and with the right spiritual atmosphere for the purpose. In some GRIMOIRES, the magician was instructed to have a new-forged sword and dagger as well as a wand of hazel, cut at sunrise. Then the magic circle was drawn out. This could be accomplished by various means, of which the most common was to draw out a PENTAGRAM or other significant shape on the ground or floor, which would serve to contain or trap the spirit; the magic circle, nine feet (2.74 metres) in diameter with an inner circle eight feet (2.44 metres) in diameter, with pentagrams and words of power drawn and written in the rim, was another. When all was prepared, the magician proceeded to call out its name or names, bidding it to appear, usually accompanied by INCANTATIONS. When in public, invocations were normally carried out in dark or dusk, often with the flickering light of a fire or candles, all of which aided the sense of mystery and sometimes convinced people that they saw that which was not actually there.

ISHTAR
One of the ancient Babylonian names for the goddess regarded as the equivalent of Venus.

J

JUDAIC MYSTERIES *see* MYSTERIES.

JUDGE, WILLIAM *see* THEOSOPHY.

JUNG, CARL GUSTAV (1875–1961)
Swiss psychiatrist. He began his career as a follower of
Sigmund Freud but split with him after challenging his concentration on sex. Jung's theory of the 'collective unconscious', a sort of vast reservoir in the unconscious mind filled
with memories and instincts common to all humans, and his
use of the term 'archetype' to denote an image or symbol
drawn from this store, have been highly influential.

K

KABBALAH

The word 'Kabbalah' is derived from the Hebrew root *kbl*, 'to receive, to accept', and in many cases is used synonymously with 'tradition'. Kabbalah is the Jewish mystical tradition, especially the system of esoteric mystical speculation and practice that developed during the twelfth and thirteenth centuries. Kabbalistic interest, at first confined to a select few, became the preoccupation of large numbers of Jews following their expulsion from Spain (1492) and Portugal (1495).

Like every other Jewish religious expression, Kabbalah was based on the Old Testament revelation but was enormously developed and expanded. The revealed text was interpreted with the aid of various hermeneutic techniques. Of the many methods available, the Kabbalists most frequently used three forms of letter and number symbolism: GEMATRIA, notarikon and temurah. The Kabbalah is very old, dating back to at least the first century AD, and much of its knowledge was passed on orally within the priesthood or within groups of the priesthood. The major written texts date from the twelfth and thirteenth centuries. The classic document of the Kabbalistic tradition, the *Zohar* (Book of Light), was compiled by Moses de Leon about 1290. The doctrine of creation was built on a theory of emanations and asserted that the world derived from the transcendent and unknowable God through a series of increasingly material manifestations (*sephirot*). The sephirot form the central image of Kabbalistic meditation, the Sephirothic Tree of Life, which describes the path of descent from the divine to the material realm and the path of ascent to the highest level of spirituality. Each sephirot is a level of attainment in knowledge, corresponding to energy centres in the body, and is also divided into four interlocking sections or 'Worlds', which constitute the cosmos: emanation (*Atziluth*), creation (*Briah*), formation (*Yetzirah*), and action or making (*Assiyah*). Through contemplation and meditation, similar to Eastern yogic disciplines, the Kabbalist ascends the tree of life. The sephirot also comprise the sacred, unknowable and unspeakable personal name of God: YHVH (Yahweh), the Tetragrammaton. So sacred is the Tetragrammaton that other names, such as Elohim and Jehovah, are substituted in its place in scripture.

A more systematic presentation of the basic doctrine is contained in Moses Cordovero's *Pardes rimmonim* (*Garden of Pomegranates*, 1548). Kabbalah was a major influence in the development of Hasidism and still has adherents among Hasidic Jews. The Kabbalah, with its amulets, incantations, demonology, seals, and letter and number mysticism, had a profound influence on Western magical tradition. The Tetragrammaton especially was held in great awe for its power over all things in the universe, including demons.

KARMA

A term, derived from the Sanskrit for 'deed', which describes the fundamental concept in Hinduism and Buddhism that thoughts and deeds determine the consequences of one's life and rebirth. Karma may therefore loosely be described as the law of consequences. In a popular sense, karma is sometimes regarded as the Eastern equivalent of the Western 'destiny' or 'fate', but this is an erroneous view. Karma is properly regarded as the fruit of actions in a previous lifetime, which determines the conditions of a life in a subsequent incarnation; this is quite different from the Western concept of destiny, which is not necessarily connected with deeds of a previous existence. Karma can be either good or bad, with relative consequences, and is generally viewed as inescapable, although various techniques of meditation and chanting exist to try to mitigate it.

KING'S EVIL

Up to the early eighteenth century it was believed that the touch of the king's hand could cure the disease scrofula (tuberculosis of the lymphatic glands). It is recorded that during his reign King Charles II touched over 92,000 of his subjects.

KIRK, ROBERT (c.1644–1692)

This Scottish clergyman is author of a strange book, *The Secret Commonwealth*, published in 1691. It is an account of his dealings with the kingdom of the fairies and also those of other people from his parish of Aberfoyle, where many seemed gifted with SECOND SIGHT.

KIRLIAN PHOTOGRAPHY

Named after Semyan Kirlian, an inventor and electrician from Krasnodar, Russia, this is a controversial technique for photographing objects in the presence of a high-frequency, high-voltage, low-amperage electrical field, the photographs of which show glowing, multicoloured emanations said to be AURAS or biofields. There is no evidence that Kirlian photography is a paranormal phenomenon. Some researchers say it reveals a physical form of psychic energy. Others believe that it reveals the ETHERIC BODY, one of the layers of the AURA believed to permeate all living things, and that an understanding of this energy will lead to greater insights into medicine, psychology, psychic healing, PSI and DOWSING. Critics say the technique shows nothing more than a discharge of electricity, which can be produced under certain conditions.

Kirlian used his own hand for his first experiment and photographed a strange glow radiating from the fingertips. He and his wife, Valentina, a biologist, experimented with photographing both live and inanimate subjects. Their work was brought to the attention of the West in the 1960s, and response in the scientific community was mixed. Kirlian photos are said to reveal health and emotion by changes in the brightness, colours and patterns of the light. Experiments in the 1970s at the University of California showed changes in a plant's glow when approached by a human hand and pricked. When part of a leaf was cut off, a glowing outline of the amputated portion still appeared on film. Subsequent research found that the glow around humans similarly reflected changes in emotional state. Psychic healers and Uri GELLER were photographed with flares of light streaming from their fingertips when engaged in their respective activities. Some

Kirlian enthusiasts consider the phantom leaf phenomenon as evidence for the existence of an etheric body. However, critics say the phenomenon disproves Kirlian photography altogether – if there really was a biofield, then the aura should disappear when an organism dies. Supporters nonetheless foresee applications of Kirlian photography in diagnostic medicine.

KNIGHTS TEMPLAR *see* ORDER OF THE KNIGHTS TEMPLAR.

KNIGHTS HOSPITALLERS (Knights of St John of Jerusalem) *see* HOSPITALLERS, KNIGHTS.

KIRSHNAMUTRI *see* THEOSOPHY.

KUNDALINI
The energy of consciousness which normally lies dormant near the root CHAKRA at the base of the spine, unless released through spiritual meditation or yoga techniques to elevate consciousness or provide mystical illumination. The term is derived from a Sanskrit word meaning approximately 'serpent energy', and the awakening of this serpent fire is arduous and filled with danger. The power of kundalini is claimed to be awesome and beyond description. The term is used by occultists in reference to one of the three fundamental solar forces in our planetary system.

In its human context, kundalini is the serpent fire or the serpent power that wreaks havoc on any individual who attempts to tamper with its workings without a sufficient occult knowledge of moral discipline. It is an energy sometimes used by black magicians (*see* BLACK MAGIC) who seek to further their malevolent aims through other individuals. Clairvoyant vision sees the activated kundalini as a kind of liquid fire rushing in a sort of spiral through the chakras of the body.

LABYRINTH

The concept of the labyrinth is central to esoteric or occult thinking. It is a dark underground maze of tunnels leading to a secret central cell where some tremendous and dangerous mystery is concealed. The first labyrinth is said to have been constructed by DAEDALUS for King Minos on the Greek island of Crete. At its heart lived the Minotaur, a terrifying creature with the head of a bull and the body of a man, that fed on the flesh of boys and maidens. It is symbolic of secret knowledge and its dangers. The fascination of the Egyptian pyramids for those of an occult turn of mind has much to do with their secret passages, enigmatic inscriptions and buried treasures. *See also* MAZES.

LAMIA

The name of a legendary queen of Libya, turned into a monstrous serpentine spirit, later became a synonym for a witch, especially for one who assumes a beautiful female form to marry and then returns to her demon shape.

LEMNISCATE

An occult symbol, a figure of eight laid on its side (∞), which is used as a reference for eternity.

LEMURIA

A legendary lost continent of the Indian Ocean, said to be the original Garden of Eden and the cradle of the human race. The theory of the existence of Lemuria arose in the nineteenth century, when natural scientists sought to explain Darwin's theory of evolution of similar species from a common ancestor. It was suggested that a land bridge once existed during the Eocene Age from the Malay Archipelago to the south coast of Asia and Madagascar, thus connecting India to southern Africa. The theory explained why such animals as the lemur are found primarily on Madagascar and in parts of Africa but also in India and the Malay Archipelago – hence 'Lemuria'. Occultists applied the term to an ancient continent which was the main centre of activity in the early history of humanity.

Madame Helena P. BLAVATSKY, cofounder of THEOSOPHY, believed that Lemuria had been inhabited by the Third Root Race of humankind, whom she described as fifteen-feet-tall (4.57 metres), brown-skinned hermaphrodites with four arms; some had a third eye in the back of the skull. Their bizarre feet, with protruding heels, enabled them to walk either forwards or backwards. Their eyes were set far apart in their flat faces so that they could see sideways. They had highly developed psychic powers and communicated by telepathy. Their continent, which covered most of the southern hemisphere, broke up and was destroyed – only fragments were left, such as modern Madagascar, the Seychelles, Easter Island and

Australia. The Lemurians migrated to ATLANTIS, where they evolved into the Fourth Root Race. Like the Lemurians, the Atlanteans fled the destruction of their own continent, spreading to other lands and starting the present Fifth Root Race.

Philosopher and occultist Rudolf STEINER, using information he said came from the Akashic Records (*see* AKASHA), said Lemuria extended from Ceylon to Madagascar and had included parts of southern Asia and Africa. He also described the Lemurians as the telepathic Third Root Race, who initially had no memory. The goal of Lemurians was to develop will and clairvoyant power of imagination in order to control the forces of nature. Lemuria was destroyed by volcanic activity.

LEO
The fifth sign of the ZODIAC.

dates: 23 July to 23 August.

origin and glyph: it probably originated in ancient Egypt, from the constellation; the glyph resembles the lion's tail.

ruling planet and groupings: Sun; masculine, fixed, fire.

typical traits: Leonians tend to be generous, creative and yet proud individuals who nevertheless need to keep a tight rein on themselves to avoid becoming overbearing. The creative nature needs to find an outlet in whatever guise, and it is common for Leonians to become organisers, with confidence and energy, although beneath that they may be rather nervous. The possible risk is that Leonians may end up taking over and feel they always know best, so they must learn to listen to the views of other people. They can also display a temper, if only briefly, and are prone to panic if things go badly wrong. However, they generally regain control of the situation quickly. Their impatience and tendency to go over the top are countered by the abundance of their positive qualities.

family: to their partners Leonians will be affectionate, but their strong will and urge to lead can make them rather domineering. However, they can be very sensitive, and criticism can cut deeply.

As parents, Leonians understand and encourage their children and will do anything to ensure they are not unhappy. However, they are not over-compliant and often associate with traditional values when it comes to behaviour and education.

Leo children tend to have an outgoing and bright personality, but they must not be allowed to be bossy towards other children, nor must their stubborn streak be allowed to develop. However, any criticism must be levelled in such a way as not to dent the rather fragile Leo self-confidence.

business: whatever their occupation or position, Leo individuals will work hard, in part because they are happier when they have people working for them. For many, luxury or glamour will appeal, and if they can achieve this through their employment then so much the better. As such, they may turn to acting, sport or working in the jewellery trade. They will often go for highly paid jobs, which they equate with status, but, equally, they make good employers, expecting the best of their employees but generous in return.

wider aspects: the Leonian is better leading rather than following and excels where generalities rather than attention to detail are accepted.

associations: *colour* – gold and scarlet; *flowers* – marigold, sunflower; *gemstone* – ruby; *trees* – citrus, walnut, olive; *food* – honey and cereals, most meats and rice.

LEPRECHAUN *see* CLURICAUNE.

LEVI, ELIPHAS (1810–1875)

The pen-name of Adolphe-Louis Constant, a French occultist, born in Paris, who became a priest but was eventually defrocked for his interest in the esoteric. A commentator and historian rather than an active practitioner, he nevertheless participated in many ritual events and sought to raise the spirit of the centuries-dead magician Apollonius of Tyana, as described in his book *Transcendental Magic*. Levi wrote a number of books on occult themes, including *A History of Magic*. He was a believer in the 'secret doctrine' that links all occult beliefs. His books were very influential. Aleister CROWLEY was to claim that he was the reincarnation of Levi.

LEVIATHAN

The word 'Leviathan' in Hebrew means approximately 'that which gathers itself into folds' or 'that which is drawn out'. There is much confusion about the translation of the word in its Biblical context, but it seems to refer to some huge animal, almost certainly linked with water. Some translators think the word might refer to a crocodile, others that it is a whale or even a large ship. The Leviathan of the English poet William Blake (1757–1827) was a coiled sea serpent. *See also* DEMONIC SINS.

LEVITATION

A phenomenon of PSYCHOKINESIS (PK), in which objects, people, animals and so on rise into the air without known physical means and float or fly about. Levitations are said to occur in mediumship, mystical trance, MAGIC, bewitchment, HAUNTINGS and POSSESSION. Christianity and Islam record numerous cases of levitation. In the first century, SIMON MAGUS is said to have levitated himself in a challenge to St Peter, as proof of his magical powers. According to legend, Peter prayed to God that Simon's deception be stopped, and Simon fell to earth and was killed. Roman Catholic hagiography includes many cases of levitations among saints. Levitation is also recorded in Hinduism and Buddhism, and the Ninja warriors of Japan also reportedly had this ability.

During the Middle Ages and Renaissance, it was common to blame any unusual phenomena upon WITCHCRAFT, FAIRIES, GHOSTS or DEMONS. Levitation was, and still is, commonly reported in demonic possession cases. Similarly, POLTERGEIST cases and hauntings are sometimes characterised by levitating. At the height of SPIRITUALISM in the late nineteenth century, certain mediums were famous for their alleged levitations. Daniel Dunglas HOME reportedly did so many times over forty years. In 1868 he was seen levitating out of a third-storey window; he floated back indoors through another window. Although Home was never exposed as a fraud, many other mediums were discovered to 'levitate' objects with hidden wires and contraptions. According to sceptics, most levitation may be explained by hallucination, HYPNOSIS or fraud.

LEY LINES
Alignments and patterns of powerful, invisible earth energy said to connect various sacred sites, such as churches, temples, stone circles, megaliths, holy wells, burial sites, and

other locations of spiritual or magical importance. The existence of leys is controversial. If they do exist, their true age and purpose remain a mystery. Controversy over them has existed since 1925, when Alfred Watkins, an English beer salesman and amateur antiquarian, published his research and theory in his book, *The Old Straight Track*. Watkins suggested that all holy sites and places of antiquity were connected by a pattern of lines he called 'leys'. Mounds, barrows, tumuli, stones, stone circles, crosses, churches built on pagan sites, legendary trees, castles, mottes and baileys, moats, hillforts, earthworks and holy wells were all thought to stand in alignment. Using the Ordnance Survey, Watkins claimed that the leys were the 'old straight tracks' that crossed the landscape of prehistoric Britain and represented all types of early human activities. After Watkins's theory was published, public fascination with leys remained high until the 1940s, when it began to decline. Interest revived in the 1960s and 1970s, as part of the NEW AGE movement. While Britain has been the chief site of investigation, there also is interest in France, the United States, Peru and Bolivia.

Many archaeologists and other scientists dispute the existence of leys and say the theory originated by Watkins was contrived because Watkins aligned secular and sacred sites from different periods of history. Even ley enthusiasts are divided into differing camps. Some hold that the prehistoric alignments can be statistically validated. Others agree but say that alignments continued in historical periods. Still others contend that leys mark paths of some sort of earth energy that can be detected by DOWSING and perhaps was sensed by early humans. The energy is compared to the flow of *ch'i*, the universal life force identified in ancient Chinese philosophy. Points where the ley energy paths intersect are said to be prone to anomalies such as earth lights and POLTERGEIST phenomena and reported sightings of UFOs (one theory suggests that the paths are navigational aids to extraterrestrial spacecraft). These energy leys, however, do not necessarily coincide with physical alignments of sites. Despite the controversy, ley researchers hope at least to come to a better understanding of ancient sacred sites and of the people who built them.

LIBRA

The seventh sign of the ZODIAC.

dates: 23 September to 23 October.

origin and glyph: The element of the scales may have several origins, possibly from their use in weighing harvests; the glyph is similar to a yoke.

ruling planet and groupings: Venus; masculine, cardinal and air.

typical traits: Librans are true to their origin – they are always trying to achieve a balance, whether between views, negotiating parties, or in their own environment. In many instances, because they prefer not to take one side or the other, they sit in the middle, and this indecision can be their greatest fault. Turned to positive effect, by combining their desire to balance with their undoubted charm, Librans make fine 'diplomats' and can often settle an argument to everyone's satisfaction. They are also easy-going and like quiet surroundings at home or work, but although they may appear vulnerable, they are in fact quite tough and ensure that they follow their own plans.

family: in relationships with a partner, Librans can be complete romantics and regard this relationship as very important, so much so that even the Libran indecisiveness can be overcome for a time.

They tend to fit well into the domestic scene, being quite capable of organising the household with their usual equable approach to all things, including money.

Librans make kind parents, although they must ensure that they are strong-willed and insist upon children doing as they are told. The Libran indecision might irritate some children, and every effort should be made to answer a child's queries. Children with this Sun sign tend to be charming and affable, and are often popular at school. Indecision and laziness should be identified and wherever possible overcome.

business: as mentioned, the tact and evenhandedness of Librans make them ideal as diplomats, in public relations, or any profession requiring these qualities. Their appreciation of art and beauty lends itself to a career in the arts or literature, and fashion, beauty and related professions are all possibilities for them. Although they like to work with other people, especially those of a like mind, they are sufficiently ambitious to reach for the top, although any isolation that this might produce would be unwelcome.

wider aspects: Librans work well anywhere where there are pleasant surroundings that are well ordered.

associations: *colour* – blues and pinks; *flowers* – bluebells, large roses; *gemstone* – sapphire; *trees* – ash, apple; *food* – cereals, most fruits and spices.

LILITH
This fierce female spirit, probably a Babylonian deity in origin, is supposed to be especially hostile to children and to pregnant women. In Talmudic legend she is a wife of Adam before Eve. In other legends she is the wife of Cain. In all cases she appears as a negative spirit of isolation, rejection and vengeance.

LIMBO
In Christianity, the abode after death for the souls of the unbaptised and those who have not offended by personal acts.

LIMBO OF THE LOST *see* BERMUDA TRIANGLE.

LONGINUS
The traditional name of the Roman soldier who pierced Christ with his spear during the Crucifixion, taken from the fifth-century Gospel of Nicodemus. The spear itself is the focus of occult legend.

LUCIFER
In demonology Lucifer is the celestial being wrongly equated with SATAN (probably as a result of a misreading of Isaiah 14:12). The general view, adopted in the literary tradition, is that Satan was called Lucifer before the Fall from Heaven. At all events, the name has been adopted in esoteric circles to represent the modern equivalent of the being of the Sun (originally named Ormuzd in the Zoroastrian dualism), opposed by the darkness, the Prince of Lies, who was called Angra Mainyu, in occultism called Ahriman.

LUCKY AND UNLUCKY DAYS *see* EGYPTIAN DAYS.

LYCANTHROPY
The hallucination that a person can be transformed into an animal. The term comes from the Greek *lukos*, 'wolf', and *anthropos*, 'man', and stories of such a metamorphosis are present in Greek myth and European folklore. It was common belief in late medieval Europe that witches could transform themselves into animals in order to wander at night and attack and devour humans to satisfy their blood lust, and then return to human form.

LYONESSE
The land, now submerged apart from the Scilly Isles, that lay to the West of Cornwall in legendary times. In some versions of the Arthurian legend, this was King Arthur's birthplace.

MAGIC

The use of a certain ritual action to bring about the intervention of a supernatural force, either in human affairs or in the natural environment, for a specific purpose. Magic has existed universally since ancient times and varies in form from primary rituals involving the well-being of an entire community to minor, peripheral, private acts of magic. All forms of magic are traditionally secret arts taught only to initiates, although in some cultures magical knowledge can sometimes be bought and sold or can be passed on through inheritance. A distinction is usually made between BLACK MAGIC, used destructively to bring misfortune or death, and white magic, which is used to ward off such attacks as well as to prevent natural calamities. In itself magic is not good or evil – it is the magician's intentions that make the difference.

The very earliest forms of magic were designed to produce some desired effect, such as rituals for successful hunting. This simple magic, also called sorcery, involved practices such as tying and untying knots, blood sacrifices, and sticking pins in wax images or little dolls or poppets. Sorcery is also called sympathetic magic – by imitating the desired result, it will happen in reality. Harmful sympathetic magic usually requires some personal effect of the victim, such as a lock of hair, a fingernail or article of clothing. It is also important that the victim be aware of the spell, which increases the likelihood of a successful result. Magical acts may be performed by individuals on their own behalf or by a magician with specialised knowledge of the rites that may be consulted. In some societies, associations of magical specialists exist. Magical practitioners may be called witch doctors, wizards, diviners, witches, wise women, cunning women, and so on.

By the Middle Ages in Europe, magical arts had become divided between low magic, such as sorcery, and high magic, which meant exploring the esoteric traditions of the KABBALAH and HERME-TICA, often through elaborate ceremonial magic (*see* FREEMASONRY, ORDER OF THE KNIGHTS TEMPLAR, ROSICRUCIANS). In ceremonial magic the aim of the ritual is to commune with God or a deity to achieve a higher consciousness. The spiritual and mystical elements of hermetic knowledge and the Jewish KABBALAH were aimed at facilitating the communication between human beings, spirits and the Divine at different levels of spiritual consciousness. Magic was discredited by the Scientific Revolution in the seventeenth and eighteenth centuries, but interest revived in the nineteenth century and various occult societies and magical fraternities were established (*see* CROWLEY). Modern neo-pagan WITCHCRAFT (or Wicca), includes both low sorcery (but not black magic or blood sacrifice) and high ceremonial.

MAGIC SQUARE

A magic square is a square array of numbers with the property that the sum of each row, each column and each diagonal is the same. Magic squares have been found in ancient writings from many parts of the world, and in some cultures they were thought to possess magical or supernatural powers. An n-by-n magic square (magic square of order n) contains n rows and n columns of numbers, which make up its n x n (n squared) elements. A magic square remains a magic square if the same number is added to each element or if each element is multiplied by the same number. Adding corresponding elements of two magic squares produces another magic square.

MAGE

An archaic English word for a magician, from MAGUS.

MAGUS

Originally a member of the priestly caste in ancient Persia; its plural form is Magi (as in the Magi who sought the infant Christ). In their rites were elements of SHAMANISM – they appear to have had no temples and performed their rituals on mountain tops – and early Hindu thinking, including that of reincarnation. The term is now commonly used for a possessor of occult wisdom; also in the English form of mage. *See* SIMON MAGUS.

MAHATMA

A term derived from a Sanskrit word meaning 'great one', used in occult terms to refer to the true masters of esoteric knowledge, who have achieved perfection and are suited to act as gurus and teachers to humanity. *See* THEOSOPHY.

MALEFICIA

A word carried over into Medieval literature from the Latin for 'evil doings' and applied to misfortunes and calamities of all kinds for which no immediate causal explanation might be given. Maleficia became inextricably woven into the idea of WITCHCRAFT and with the work of the DEVIL, to a point where the word became a synonym for 'witch'.

MALLEUS MALEFICARUM

Literally, 'the hammer of witches', a book published in 1486 by two members of the Inquisition, the period from the fifteenth to the seventeenth centuries when the Roman Catholic Church sought out and punished heretics. In its time it was considered the leading work on the identification of witches and their practices. It identified four prime points that characterised the witch – renunciation of the true Catholic faith, devotion to evil, offering unbaptised children to the DEVIL, and unbridled lust.

MAMMON

Mammon was not originally a DEMON but simply the Syrian term for 'money' or 'riches'. He entered the lists of demons in the words of Christ (Matthew 6:24). By Biblical exegesis and popular misunderstanding he developed a variety of corrupt names which flourished in a number of demonologies, and eventually he emerged in popular consciousness as the demon of money or (more precisely) the demon of love of money. *See also* DEMONIC SINS.

MANDALA

Derived from the Sanskrit for 'circle', a mandala is a symbolic diagram of the universe used for ritual purposes in Buddhism and Hinduism. It is also frequently represented in Chinese, Japanese and Tibetan Buddhist art, and has appeared in various forms in Christianity, GNOSTICISM and other religions, as well as in mythology and ALCHEMY. The mandala generally consists of a group of cosmic deities (or their symbols or associated magic syllables) that are arranged in one or more circles surrounded by a square and orientated toward the points of the compass. Some of the earliest mandalas were laid out architecturally, as at the Buddhist temple of Borobudur in Java and the Samye monastery in Tibet. They were also frequently drawn in powder on the ground for use in initiation rites. From the ninth century, mandalas were painted on walls or on cloth or paper. Images of mandalas are often visualised in the mind during meditation practices. The Swiss psychologist Carl Gustav JUNG considered the mandala to be what he termed an archetype, a universally occurring pattern associated with the mythological representation of the self. In modern psychotherapies the mandala is used as a therapeutic tool.

MANDRAKE
The root of the mandragora plant often takes a forked shape, vaguely resembling the human form. For this reason the plant was invested with human qualities and it was supposed to scream when pulled from the ground. Its narcotic properties also helped its magic reputation. Mandrake roots were often carved to enhance their human appearance and used as charms and amulets, often associated with fertility.

MATERIALISATION
The appearance of apparently solid objects and spirit entities

out of thin air. Materialisations were a popular phenomenon during the height of spiritualist seances in the late nineteenth and early twentieth centuries (*see* SPIRITUALISM). Many instances of materialisation were observed and even photographed during this period, including the materialisation of objects (*see* APPORT), such as cups, coins and flowers; animal spirits, body parts, such as human hands, and even complete spirit forms. Some mediums exhibited the ability to dematerialise and then rematerialise parts of themselves. The fact that seances often occurred in darkened rooms made it easy for fraudulent mediums to fake materialisations, using sleight-of-hand or various ingenious stage props. Materialisations of complete spirits, for example, usually turned out to be the medium himself or herself, wrapped in muslin or wearing a more elaborate disguise. Some mediums, however, were never successfully exposed as frauds.

MAZES
Like LABYRINTHS, mazes are physical expressions of secret knowledge. To reach the centre you have to know, or work out, the way. Mazes are found not only in gardens. Ancient mazes can be found traced in the ground, like the turf-maze at Saffron Walden in Suffolk, or on the floors of churches, like San Miniato in Florence (this church is prolific in occult symbolism). Dance mazes, like Julian's Bower at Alkborough, Humberside, England, are different in that their pattern is designed to be followed in a ritualistic dance pattern that inevitably leads to the centre.

MEDICINE MEN
In the American Indian tradition, 'medicine' stands for the

attributes, good or bad, that are inherent in all objects and can be interpreted and used by the skilled practitioner. The object could be a stone or a feather, or an animal. The abilities of medicine men went far beyond this, however. Early European explorers witnessed the 'shaking tent' phenomenon. The medicine man erects a small wigwam, supported by stout poles, enters it naked and begins a series of incantations that evoke the earth spirits. During this process the wigwam shakes and shudders, apparently of its own accord, and sparks or lights are seen to come out from the top. The medicine man was supposed to depart from his body and commune with the spirits, thereby gaining important knowledge for the tribe.

Medicine men were known for their ability to walk on red-hot stones and cinders without injury, and even to put red-hot coals into their mouths. They claimed the ability to work both good and harm on other people at a great distance and practised many forms of clairvoyance also known in Europe, including SCRYING and gazing into the surface of a bowl of water.

MEDIUM

A term applied to those who allegedly have the ability, conscious or unconscious, to communicate with dead spirits, perform paranormal feats and channel the universal life force for healing (*see* CHANNELLING). Mediums have been known by various names, such as ORACLE, soothsayer, wizard, cunning woman, wise woman, witch, medicine man, sorcerer, shaman, fortune-teller, witch doctor, mystic, priest, prophet and channeller. Mental mediumship uses techniques such as CLAIRAUDIENCE or AUTOMATIC WRITING to communicate, whilst physical mediumship involves RAPPINGS, APPORTS, LEVITATION or movement of objects and other paranormal phenomena. Mediums usually claim to communicate with spirits through one or more entities called 'controls' (or spirit guides), which usually remain permanently with the medium. Prevailing theory among parapsychologists holds that controls are not external spirits but secondary aspects of the medium's own personality that become externalised. *See* SPIRITUALISM.

MELUSINE
A witch-princess from French legend. Having imprisoned her father for offending her mother, she was condemned to be turned into a serpent from the waist down every seventh day. She married Raymond, count of Lusignan, and forbade him ever to see her on a Saturday, but one day he hid and saw her transformed shape. After that, he kept her hidden in a dungeon until her death. The name has become the word for a type: the shape-changing fairy woman or melusina.

MEN IN BLACK
A mysterious phenomenon associated with sightings of uni-dentified flying objects (UFOs). Some individuals who claim to have seen UFOs, or to have been abducted or in some other way involved with extraterrestrial beings, also claim to have been visited later by Men in Black (MIB) – men dressed in dark clothes – who discourage the individuals from publicising their experiences. According to UFO enthusiasts, one of the earliest cases of an MIB visit occurred in September 1953. Albert K. Bender, a factory clerk of Bridgeport, Connecticut, and a UFO enthusiast, had figured out parts of the origin of flying saucers and sent his theory off to a 'trusted

friend'. Soon afterwards, three men dressed in black appeared, with his letter in hand. They told him 'the real story', and he became ill. Bender, apparently to 'save mankind', kept the details to himself and gave up UFO research. There have been various reports of MIB visits since, mostly in the United States but also elsewhere, including Europe, Australia and South Africa. *See also* FORTEAN PHENOMENA.

MEPHISTOPHELES
The evil tempter of FAUST, and a name for the DEVIL. The name is from Greek, meaning 'one who hates the light'.

MERLIN
In Arthurian legend Merlin was a sorcerer and counsellor of Uther Pendragon and his son, Arthur. It was on Merlin's advice that Uther established the Round Table and found his true heir through the sword-in-the-stone test. Merlin was said to be a son of the DEVIL, who had been baptised and so turned his powers to good account. He disappeared forever when the Lady of the Lake, using magic that he had taught her, imprisoned him in an enchanted thorn bush. Merlin represents an amalgamation of a Celtic sky deity and a Welsh or British bard who lived about AD 500.

MESMER, FRANZ ANTON (1734–1815)
An Austrian physician who believed the human nervous system to be magnetised, just as the Earth is, a universal life force which he called 'animal magnetism'. He believed that all space is permeated by a psychic 'ether' that is affected by the CELESTIAL BODIES. If these movements are prevented, then sickness results. Practising first in Vienna and then in Paris,

Mesmer developed a therapeutic regime using iron magnets, which he believed helped to restore the magnetic balance in the life-force of sick patients. His methods included laying on of hands, staring fixedly into a subject's eyes and slowly waving his hands or a magnetic wand in front of the patient. He attracted a large following who believed that animal magnetism – or mesmerism, as it was popularly called – was a cure for all manner of physical and mental ailments. Although often accused by contemporaries of being a magician and charlatan, 'mesmerism', in the form of modern hypnosis, has now become an accepted psychotherapeutic technique. Mesmer's main contribution to occultism is his awareness of natural forces and the need to allow them freedom.

MIB *see* MEN IN BLACK.

MIRROR

Since ancient times, mirrors – as well as all smooth, reflective surfaces – have been used for DIVINATION, MAGIC and repelling evil. They have also been greatly feared for their power to steal the soul. In recent times, mirrors have been used as tools in psychic development to increase CLAIRVOYANCE and to gain knowledge of so-called past lives. Divination with mirrors is call crystalomancy, catoptromancy and SCRYING. In the West, magic mirrors were particularly popular from the Middle Ages to the nineteenth century. They were used by all classes of society, but especially by magicians, witches, sorcerers and cunning men and women. Catherine de Medici and Henry IV often consulted their magic mirrors. Dr John DEE, the royal magician to Queen Elizabeth I, used a crystal egg and a black obsidian mirror. In more recent times, mirrors as magic tools have fallen out of widespread popular fashion but are still used by diviners, psychics and students of psychism. Mirrors are more commonly used for divination in the East than in the West. In parts of India, preparation for mirror divination involves rituals of fasting, prayer and the perfuming of the mirrors. In many tribal societies, the reflection is believed to be the soul. Exposing the soul in a mirror or a reflecting surface makes it vulnerable to danger and death. A common belief in many cultures holds that a person who sees his or her reflection will soon die. This is the basis for the Greek myth of Narcissus, who looked upon his reflection in the water and pined and died. The ancient Greeks also believed that dreaming of seeing one's reflection was an omen of death. A worldwide folklore custom is the removal of mirrors from sick rooms, in case the mirror should draw out the soul of a weakened person, and the turning or removal of mirrors following a death in the house. According to superstition, whoever looks into a mirror following a death will also die.

Mirrors are associated with evil. In Russian folklore they are the invention of the Devil and will draw souls out of bodies. In other superstitions, if one looks into the mirror long enough at night or by candlelight, one will see the Devil; thus it is advisable to cover up mirrors in the bedroom at night. The candlelight is not advisable because fire is the element of spirit and attracts the unseen. Witches and vampires cast no reflections in mirrors. The look of the EVIL EYE will shatter a mirror or poison its surface. Conversely, mirrors may be used to protect against evil. They can reflect the evil eye. In the seventeenth century, it was fashionable in Europe to wear small mirrors in hats.

Numerous superstitions surround mirrors. Breaking one means bad luck for seven years, or disaster or death. A mirror that falls and breaks of its own accord is an omen of impending death in the house. A girl who gazes at the Moon's reflection in a mirror will learn her wedding day; if performed on Hallowe'en, the ritual will reveal a vision of her future husband. Students of the occult use mirrors to look into the world of spirits. Gazing into one supposedly reveals visions of spirit guides and helps one gain auric sight, the ability to see the AURA. Some believe that the face changes produced by staring into a mirror are images of past lives. Mirrors painted black on the convex side are considered an excellent tool for developing clairvoyance.

MITHRAIC MYSTERIES *see* MYSTERIES.

MOON
The Moon is associated with WITCHCRAFT, MAGIC and SORCERY, and is considered to be the source of witches' power. The ancient witches of Thessaly were said to have the power to draw the Moon down from the sky at their command. A symbolic ritual of drawing down the Moon is still performed in modern WITCHCRAFT. Witches hold their meetings, called 'circles' or 'esbats', and perform their magic spells in accordance with lunar phases. The waxing Moon is propitious for growth, achievement, good fortune, and healing spells. The waning Moon is propitious for banishing spells and the undoing of harm and negative influences. The Moon itself is believed to cast a spell; one may become moonstruck beneath its silvery rays. The term 'mania', derived from 'moon', means ecstatic revelation; 'lunacy' means possessed by the

spirit of Luna. Nights of the full Moon provide the greatest power for magic and the world of spirit. In folklore, those cursed by LYCANTHROPY are said to turn into WEREWOLVES under the spell of the full Moon. In ASTROLOGY, the Moon exerts a powerful force in horoscopes and in daily affairs. As the Moon moves through the ZODIAC, different creative forces are brought into play, and when the Moon is between signs it is a time of uncertainty and instability.

MOTHMAN *see* FORTEAN PHENOMENA.

MYSTERIES
Secret religious cults that flourished during the Hellenistic period, involving adoration of various deities and rites of spiritual transformation and rebirth. In a broader sense, the term 'mysteries' is also applied to esoteric teachings and the rites of secret societies outside the classical world. 'Mystery' derives from the Greek *myein*, 'to close', and refers to the closing of the lips or the eyes. The *mystes*, or initiate, was required to keep the secrets of the cult. The content of the rites remains a secret, but the large numbers who underwent the initiation, often lasting several days, were promised eternal life in the afterworld through rebirth or redemption.

The Eleusinian mysteries, the most popular and influential of the Greek cults, centred on the worship of Persephone and her mother, Demeter, the grain goddess. The rites were intimately linked to the cycle of fertility of the Earth. The Dionysian mysteries, the second most important Hellenistic cult, centred on Dionysus (Bacchus), the Thracian bull-god and ruler of the dead and souls, who became the god of the vine and vegetation. Immortality could be obtained through communion with him in ecstatic rites apparently involving consumption of wine and the raw flesh of a sacrificed animal, and sex. In the mysteries of Isis and Osiris, the Egyptians observed a mystery play of succession, the death of a pharaoh and the succession of another, with a funeral ritual of mummification and burial in which the dead would be mystically joined in the Underworld by Osiris.

The Mithraic mysteries were a male cult of Persian origin centred on the slaying of a bull by Mithra, god of light and beneficence, which guaranteed the fruitfulness of the earth. The initiates consumed bread and water, representing the body and blood of the divine bull. Initiates were believed to be under the divine protection of Mithra, who would protect their souls from darkness. There were also Judaic and Christian mysteries. Rites of circumcision, baptism and anointing the forehead with oil may be seen to have similarities with the ancient mystery rites of initiation into a select religious community. The Jewish holy meal of Seder re-enacts a religious drama, the Exodus from Egypt.

The primary Christian mysteries are the Eucharist, the Cross and the baptism. The rite of the Eucharist involves the consumption of bread and wine as the body and blood of Christ, a means of seeking salvation through union with Christ. Goddess or Great Mother remains a hidden part of these rites, as the cup that holds the blood and wine and the womb in which the rebirth of baptism takes place. The Cross represents the scheme of the universe, the entire history of the cosmos before and after the crucifixion of Christ; it foreshadows the coming of the transfigured Christ. The baptism, the fundamental mystery, represents initiation into the divine life of the resurrected Christ. The elements and purpose of the ancient mysteries – resurrection to eternal life – have been preserved in the rites of various secret societies such as the FREEMASONS and ROSICRUCIANS.

MYSTERY HELICOPTERS *see* FORTEAN PHENOMENA.

NAMES

Names are a form of concealment as well as an expression of identity. In kabbalistic lore (*see* Kabbalah), the mighty angel Metatron has more than seventy other names. Some of them express particular aspects or functions, but others may simply be decoys. The true ADEPT would know the false or ill-taught one by the incorrect use of names in such cases. Also, certain spirits were of such power that to use their names incautiously might be likened to touching a bare electric wire. Thus DEMOGORGON was a secret name for hundreds of years. Even today, there are a host of by-names for the DEVIL. A name was felt to be more than a label; it was part of the person or being, and possession of it gave some power over its owner. Conversely, to have no name was to have no identity at all.

NAMES OF POWER

In magical theory the real name of a spirit contains the essence of its being, and simply to call out its name is to have access to its power. In the ancient world, there was a mystical belief that one name of dreadful power was the key to everything in the universe. To utter it would mean the instant end of everything. In Jewish tradition this was the name of God. For this reason, God was referred to by circumlocutory words like El (a god), Elohim (the divine spirit or spirits), Adonai (Lord), Shaddai (almighty) and Sabaoth (Lord of hosts). The Tetragrammaton (*see* KABBALAH) came closer to the true name but did not spell it out. The longest name of God is called the Shemhamphorash and is the name of seventy-two syllables that Moses used to part the Red Sea. Numerological tradition underlies many names (*see* NUMEROLOGY). Metatron, an angel, is interchangeable with Shaddai because both add up to 314.

Other names to conjure with include Agla, from the Hebrew *Aieth Gadol Leolam Adonia*, 'thou art mighty, O Lord'; Schemes Amathia, 'Sun be silent'; On, a name for the Egyptian city of Heliopolis, the centre of the Sun cult; Elion, 'god most high'. Some names of great portent have no known origin, like Siras Etas Besanar, for calling up all the spirits of hell; or Saritap Pernisox Ottarim, to make a lock spring open. *See also* INCANTATIONS.

NATURE SPIRITS

Various types of beings said to exist in nature. Belief in the existence of nature spirits is common to all cultures throughout history. They are usually attached to a specific place, such as a tree, river, plant or mountain. They come in a variety of shapes and temperaments. Some are described as human in form, others are like animals or are half-human, half animal; some are helpful, others deceitful or malevolent. They are normally invisible to humans, except to those with the gift of CLAIRVOYANCE. Elementals are a sub-class of nature spirits that are a part of the life force of all things in nature. They are ruled by ARCHANGELS and are generally regarded as benevolent. The Neo-Platonic Greeks categorised elementals according to the four ELEMENTS: Earth elementals are gnomes, Air elementals are SYLPHS, Water elementals are undines, and Fire elementals are salamanders. In the Middle Ages interest in these main groups was revived and alchemists and magicians sought to control and manipulate the forces of nature and the universe. Other elementals include elves, who live in the woods, and household spirits such as brownies, goblins and bogles. Fairies are also sometimes included in this category (*see* FAIRY).

NECROMANCY

DIVINATION by raising the spirits of the dead, one of the claimed Black Arts practised by witches and magicians. The classic case of necromancy is the Witch of Endor, described in the Bible (1 Samuel 28), who summoned the spirit of Samuel in the presence of Saul. This Biblical episode was widely accepted as irrefutable evidence for the existence of WITCHCRAFT. The idea behind necromancy was that the dead could see the future and could be conjured into describing it. It is unlike other forms of divination in that its tools are not part of the world around us, like clouds or rods or animal entrails. It goes back to legends of descents to the Underworld and visits from the dead, such as are recorded in Shakespeare's play *Hamlet,* but in its trappings and rituals it is more a branch of BLACK MAGIC than of regular divination, which relies on the person of the diviner being in tune with the phenomena he or she is assessing. Nine days of morbid and grisly preparation are required, in which the magician dresses in the burial clothes of corpses and recites the funeral service over to himself and his assistants. At midnight or dawn, the grave is opened and the corpse conjured to come out alive. In accounts of such events, the corpse is often made to speak through the mouth of one of the assistants.

NEW AGE

A term that became popular in the 1980s and is used to describe a nebulous, quasi-religious set of beliefs encompassing a wide array of notions, such as SPIRITUALISM, ASTROLOGY, mysticism, the occult, REINCARNATION, PARAPSYCHOLOGY, ecology and planetary awareness, as well as a commitment to complimentary medicine and the pseudo-scientific applications of the 'healing powers' of crystals and pyramids. New Age beliefs and practices are largely confined to the industrialised West, and the origins of the movement can be traced to the social and political unrest in the 1960s, dissatisfaction with obsessive materialism, the influence of Eastern religions, experimentation with psychedelic drugs, the development of humanistic psychology and increased eco-consciousness. Despite hostility from the popular media and the establishment, New Age ideas now permeate many areas of mainstream culture, notably in the areas of behavioural medicine, physics, psychology and even business.

NINE-KNOTTED STRING

A death-charm used by malevolent witches, in which a string was knotted nine times while charms against the enemy are uttered. It is then concealed close to the person and the knots gradually choke the life out of him or her. The mystic significance of the number Nine is notable here.

NINE WORLDS OF CREATION

In Nordic lore, the Nine Worlds form the Cosmos. They are all placed on the Web of WYRD, spun between roots and branches of the cosmic tree Yggdrasil. They are Midgard, the middle ground, or Earth; Nilheim, the land of ice and fog; Jotunheim, the land of giants; Muspellsheim, the land of fire; Vanaheim, the land of the fertility spirits; Svartalfheim, the land of the elf-smiths; Ljossalfheim, the world of the star elves, space; Helheim, the Underworld where the spinning goddess Urdr, who weaves the web, lives; and Asgard, the land of the gods.

NOSTRADAMUS, MICHAEL (1503–66)

French physician and astrologer, born in Provence, whose predictions of the future have fascinated people for centuries. Nostradamus was taught medicine at the University of Montpellier and acquired fame as a doctor by treating victims of the plague, but he eventually turned more to astrology and metaphysics. He travelled widely through Europe. In 1555 he completed the *Centuries*, a book of more than 900 predictions about the fate of France, the world and celebrated persons of his time. He became a celebrity, admired and reviled in equal measure. By his own calculation, his prophecies extended to the year 3797. The title of the book refers to the fact that the contents are arranged in sections of 100 verses each. An expanded version was published in 1558. His prophecies are written as four-lined rhymed verses (quatrains) in vague, often cryptic language. His fondness for astrology, anagrams and his penchant for sprinkling his verses with Hebrew, Latin and Portuguese words further complicate interpretation of his predictions. Some interpreters say the verses can be applied to anything, or nothing, whereas others claim that various verses foretold such occurrences as the Great Fire of London in 1666, the deaths of several monarchs, details of the French Revolution, the rise of Napoleon and Hitler, and World War II, including air battles and tank battles. Because Nostradamus included very few dates in his prophecies and because, additionally, he did not organise them into a chronological order, the verses have been constantly reinterpreted since their publication. The *Centuries* remains a classic of occult literature and hundreds of studies of it have been published.

NUMBER OF THE BEAST
The number 666 is so called from a reference in the Book of Revelation, which apparently refers to a particular man, possibly the Emperor Nero, whom the Christians had good reason to consider their arch-enemy, although other early emperors who persecuted Christians have also been suggested. Depending on whether it is written in Greek or Hebrew, it can be taken to signify Caligula or Trajan, and it has also been taken as a prophetic indication of some figure who has yet to come. The reason for triple six being given this unwelcome distinction is not clear, although it may be that since the number seven was taken as a number of perfection, this was seen as the opposite. *See* NUMEROLOGY, GEMATRIA.

NUMBERS
Numbers are of great significance in occultism because they

readily form an esoteric code and at the same time they conform to a system that cannot be altered. This point also means that occultists often see numbers as the key to understanding the universe (*see* NUMEROLOGY), seeing them as something that exists beyond human invention and manipulation. There are innumerable languages, but there is only one set of numbers. Words can be tampered with, their meanings can change, but numbers have an eternal permanency.

They have another virtue. There are basically only nine of them, even although their combinations are infinite. For this reason, occultists have evolved systems of reducing the endless variety of names into the more classifiable taxonomy of numbers. To convert any name into its defining number, there is a simple grid. First write down the numbers 1 to 9. Then under the numbers write down the 26 letters of the alphabet, in three rows of 9 and one row of 8. Write down your name, as you normally use it, together with the number equivalents for each letter. Add the numbers. If the addition comes to two figures or more, add these together and repeat the process until you reach a single figure. This, the 'digital root', is the corresponding number to your name. Occultists believe that this number is of great significance in a person's life and, if known, can give a very good indication of the individual's nature.

In a further process, you can add the vowels only, to establish what is known as your 'heart number', which is said to reveal your hidden inner nature; or the consonants only, to reveal your external nature – this is a distinction that goes back to written Egyptian and Hebrew, where the consonants only were written down. Numerologists also establish the birth number, found by adding the number values of the letters in the birth month to the actual date, so that 5 November 1980 comes out as $5 + 11 + 1 + 9 + 8 + 0 = 35 = 3 + 5 = 8$. Your birth number and your number may not harmonise with each other, and such a conflict will be expressed in your own nature. The number values, briefly expressed, are as follows:

one   – positive, single-minded, ambitious, inventive, self-centred.
two   – even-tempered, tactful, modest, indecisive.
three – bold, witty, versatile, charming, lightweight.
four   – solid, practical, efficient, rather dull, melancholic.
five   – restless, speculative, adventurous, unconventional.
six   – harmonious, domestic, reliable, loyal.
seven – scholarly, mystically inclined, withdrawn, dreamy.
eight – strong-willed, struggling, drudging, veering from success to failure.
nine   – idealistic, visionary, passionate, impulsive, unorthodox, naive.

Serious students of numbers make use of their own numbers in various ways, making use of numbers that happen to correspond, checking the numbers of potential friends or business partners, doing certain things on dates that contain their number, and so on. They do not regard the number as the product of sheer chance but as part of the harmonious working process of the entire universe.

NUMEROLOGY

A system of DIVINATION and occult practice based on the idea that the universe is mathematically constructed and that all things can be expressed in numbers, which correspond to vibrations. Because all letters, words, names, birthdates and so on can be expressed in numbers, which in turn are ascribed complex religious and mystical meanings, a person's life, personality and destiny can be determined.

Occult numerology began with PYTHAGORAS who, from certain observations in music, mathematics and astronomy, believed that all relations could be reduced to number relations ('all things are numbers'). This formed the basis of a mystical system expanded upon by later Greek philosophers. Jewish KABBALAH mysticism (*see* GEMATRIA), ancient Near Eastern religions (especially those in Babylon and Egypt) and the Hindu, Buddhist and Chinese faiths have all erected elaborate divinatory systems based on mystical numerological correspondences.

In most occult systems only the numbers 1 to 9, together with 0, are considered in any depth, for all numbers greater than 9 can be reduced to a single digit by adding the digits together. This reductionism is the main tool of numerological divination. Consider the number 642 which can be reduced to $6 + 4 + 2 = 12$ and then $1 + 2 = 3$. The number 642 is therefore equivalent to the symbolic number 3. Each number has its own characteristics and values (male/female, strong/passive, harmonious/disharmonious, and so on) and also corresponds to a letter of the alphabet. See NUMBERS. Various formulae can be applied to a person's name, birthday and birthplace to determine his or her character and destiny. Numerology is also used to determine propitious days for certain activities, such as selecting marriage partners or choosing a baby's name. There is an alternative, older form of numerology which makes use of the letters of the Hebrew alphabet.

OBE *see* OUT-OF-BODY EXPERIENCE.

OCCULTISM

The study or practice of the lore of the occult (*see* Introduction). Occultism covers a wide range of thought and activity, from the harmless to the diabolical. Its attraction is often to those who are impatient with the conventional knowledge of their times, who feel convinced that there is a group of initiates who have access to a hidden truth and who yearn to be members of such a group. For many people, occultism today is little more than a game or a diversion. Others still regard it as the means of attaining forms of knowledge and experience not available in any other way.

Modern occultism, with the aid of Jungian psychology and other developments of the twentieth century, has moved away from the obsession with death, blood and the devil that characterised so much esoteric study in the past. Most occultists are seeking to find a harmony with the forces that guide the universe and not to oppose them or seek in some theatrical way to 'control' them. Dangers and delusions still remain, however. Confused fragments of occult legend can still attract the ignorant or weak-minded and provide false justifications for all kinds of prejudice and persecution. Occultism is unstructured and not governed by any generally agreed code, and this freedom is part of its appeal. Like a lift-shaft, it provides access to the lower and the higher part of our natures. It needs to be handled with care.

OCCULT POWERS
According to the poet and mythological expert Robert Graves, one person in twenty is the possessor of occult powers. These are the people who experience 'second sight', who are capable of entering a state of deep trance and who are naturally able to tap into the streams of invisible energy that permeate the world. Many pass their lives without being aware of this gift, but it is only from this group that the fully empowered occultist can come.

OGAM *or* OGHAM
Ogam is an ancient alphabet of the Celtic languages. Many standing stones bear ogam inscriptions. The alphabet has twenty letters, in groups of five, made from straight lines cut across a single vertical stave. Although there is little direct evidence, it seems that the alphabet was used for divinatory purposes by incising the letters on the end of twigs then casting the twigs and examining the pattern in which they fell.

OLCOTT, HENRY STEEL *see* THEOSOPHY.

OMEGA
The final letter of the Greek alphabet, taken to represent the end of things, as ALPHA does the start.

OMEN
A supernatural sign or event presaging a future event. There are two basic kinds of omen: normal occurrences of nature (the hooting of owls or howling of dogs, for example), which are interpreted in a specific context to augur good or bad fortune; and unusual occurrences, such as flights of sacred birds, or eclipses or comets, that are believed to be direct manifestations of the gods. Dreams have provided omens for thousands of years. Some are obscure and have to be interpreted. Others are precognitive, such as warning of impending disasters.

ONEIROMANCY
The interpretation of dreams as a means of DIVINATION, from Greek *oneiros*, 'dream'. The method used was often the so-called 'incubatory sleep', in which a person slept in a particular building or cave, after some form of purification and possibly consuming some narcotic substance. When he or she awoke, the priests or priestesses of the place would assist in interpreting the dream. This form of divination was practised in ancient Greece but was also widely used by the Celtic peoples.

ORACLE
A method of DIVINATION and prophecy in which gods or spirits are consulted through a human medium. In ancient Greece, the voices or mediums of the oracles were sibyls, women

priests who lived in caves regarded as the shrines of deities. The most famous Greek oracles were at Dodua, where Zeus was thought to give answers through the rustling of oak leaves, and at Delphi, where Apollo supposedly spoke through a priestess. In both cases, oracular responses came so ambiguously that it was difficult to prove them wrong. A famous Roman oracle was at Cumae, where the sibyl was said to have drawn inspiration from Apollo.

ORDER OF THE KNIGHTS TEMPLAR

The Knights Templar were a military and religious order founded in Jerusalem during the Crusades. The founders were Hugh de Payns and Geoffrey de Saint-Omer, knights who in 1118 established a religious community on the ancient site of the Temple of Solomon which was dedicated to protecting pilgrims in the Holy Land. Saint Bernard of Clairvaux, head of the Cistercian order of monks, drew up the order's rules, but in 1128 Pope Honorious II officially recognised the templars as a separate order, conferring on them an unprecedented degree of autonomy. They were responsible only to the pope and not to secular rulers, were exempt from local taxes and judicial authority, and were solely responsible for clerical appointments.

The Templars were divided into knights, chaplains, sergeants and craftsmen, organised under a grand master and a general council. They wore a white cloak with a red eight-pointed cross. The Templars attracted many nobles and soon became an expert military force and a powerful, wealthy order, with branches throughout Europe. After 1291, when the crusading forces were driven from Palestine, the Templars' main activity became money-lending, and their enormous landholdings and financial strength aroused great hostility among rulers and clergy alike. It was rumoured that they had abandoned Christianity, that they worshiped a demon called BAPHOMET and indulged in a variety of perverted orgiastic and cannibalistic rituals.

In 1307, Philip IV of France, in debt to the order, charged the Templars with heresy and immorality. They were arrested and put on trial, and confessions were extracted by torture. Similar attacks were mounted against the order in Spain and England, and Pope Clement V, after initially opposing the trials, suppressed the Knights Templar by papal bull at the Council of Vienne in 1312. When the grand master, Jacques de Molay, and other leaders of the Templars retracted their forced confessions and declared their innocence and the innocence of the order, Philip had them burned at the stake at Paris in 1314. The Templars' holdings were dispersed, some going to the Knights Hospitallers and some to secular rulers, although Philip received none. It has been suggested that some leading Templars escaped and founded FREEMASONRY. Another tradition is that Templar survivors founded the ROSICRUCIANS.

ORDER OF ORIENTAL TEMPLARS
Founded by a German, Karl Kellner, in 1902 after a visit to India, this order borrowed features from the Knights Templar but its principal novelty was to incorporate some of the ideas of Tantric Yoga. In this Indian and Tibetan school, the yogi uses sexual ecstasy to create new levels of psychic intensity and spiritual power. Kellner evolved two types of ritual, one based on feasting and orgiastic sex, the other centred on restraint both in consumption and intercourse. In both the focus is on prolonging the sexual intensity rather than ending

it by a climax. For a time Aleister CROWLEY headed an English branch of the Order.

ORDER OF THE ROSY CROSS *see* ROSICRUCIANS.

ORMUZD *see* AHURA MAZDA.

OUIJA

A board and pointer used for DIVINATION and to contact the spirit world. The name comes from the French for 'yes', *oui*, and the German for 'yes', *ja*. The board, which has the letters of the alphabet, the numbers 0 to 9, and the words 'yes' and 'no' printed on it, is placed on a table. Participants rest their fingertips lightly on the pointer, a heart-shaped device with three felt-tipped legs. One person poses a question, and the pointer is then supposed to move to answer the question. Similar board-type instruments were used for divination in ancient China and Greece. In the mid-nineteenth century a similar device, the PLANCHETTE, came into use in Europe.

The modern Ouija board is marketed as a game, originally called 'Ouija Talking Board', and was developed in the late 1890s by an American, William Fuld, who sold the patent to the Parker Brothers game company in 1966. Ouija boards became popular during and after World War I, when many people were desperate to communicate with loved ones killed in the fighting. Parapsychologists regard the Ouija as a means to tap into the subconscious. Critics claim that it is dangerous in that users have no control over repressed material, which may lead to psychological trauma. Most Christian denominations condemn it as dangerous tinkering with potentially harmful occult forces and a tool of the DEVIL.

OUT-OF-BODY EXPERIENCE (OBE)

The experience of feeling separated from one's physical body and apparently being able to travel through space and perceive distant locations. Occultists also call these experiences 'astral travel' and 'astral projection'. Descriptions of out-of-body experiences are universal and have occurred throughout history, but there is no scientific evidence for them, and sceptics claim that out-of-body experiences are a product of an altered state of consciousness induced by meditation, psychological stress or drugs.

P

PALMISTRY

A method of DIVINATION and character interpretation by study-
ing the lines and bumps on the palms and fingers. This is
very ancient divinatory technique, formerly called
cheiromancy or chiromancy. The technique was very popular in the Middle Ages, practitioners believing that the lines
in the hand were stamped by occult forces and would reveal
character and destiny. The lines, digits and bumps on the
hands all have supposedly astrological correspondences,
which indicate such factors as longevity, general health, intellect, love, money, and so on. In the fifteenth century the
church banned the practice, and after the Enlightenment palmistry became little more than a parlour trick.

PARACELSUS (1493–1541)

The name coined for himself by the German physician and
alchemist Theophrastus Bombastus von Hohenheim, who was
born in Einsieden, Switzerland. Paracelsus was a medical
reformer who introduced a new concept of disease and the

use of chemical medicines. He studied at several Italian universities and began to practise medicine and surgery in the 1520s. A difficult personality, he created controversy because of his wholesale condemnation of traditional science and medicine. He never obtained a secure academic position or permanent employment. His new concept of disease emphasised its causes to be external agents that attack the body, contrary to the traditional idea of disease as an internal upset of the balance of the body's humours (yellow bile, black bile, blood and phlegm). Therapy, according to Paracelsus, was to be directed against these agents of disease, and for this he advocated the use of chemicals rather than herbs, and AL-CHEMY became the means of preparing such chemicals. In this way Paracelsus changed the emphasis of the alchemical art from chasing the elusive elixir of life, or PHILOSOPHER'S STONE, to making medicines.

PARAPSYCHOLOGY

Parapsychology is the study of the ability of the mind to perform psychic acts. Psychic phenomena, as the term is applied to the human mind, generally fall into two broad categories: extrasensory perception (ESP) and PSYCHOKINESIS (PK), or PSI, as both are collectively known. Parapsychology is an outgrowth of the SPIRITUALISM movement in the late 1800s in Great Britain and the United States. The British Society for Psychical Research, founded in 1882, and the American Society for Psychical Research, founded in 1885, both sought to establish whether mediums who conducted spiritualistic seances actually contacted the dead or were merely fakes.

Much of the early evidence cited by psychical societies and others for the existence of psychic phenomena was highly unscientific and anecdotal in nature. They included reports of premonitions and dreams, newspaper stories of spiritualistic LEVITATION, written accounts of GHOST sightings, and so on. More scientifically rigorous investigation using controlled laboratory experiments began in America in 1927, pioneered by the psychologist J. B. Rhine of Duke University in North Carolina. Rhine eventually split with the university psychology department and was allowed to form the first parapsychological laboratory in the country in 1935. Although Rhine was not the first worker in the field to use statistical methods in his investigations, his methodology was regarded as more rigorous and sophisticated than those of earlier investigators. Test subjects were ordinary people, mostly volunteers, not mediums.

In a typical CLAIRVOYANCE experiment, Rhine would seat the test subject in one building and the experimenter in another. The experimenter would shuffle a deck of Zener cards (a specially designed ESP testing deck, each card having one of five boldly printed symbols – star, square, circle, plus sign, and three wavy lines). Then the experimenter would draw a card and place it face down on the table. After a minute the experimenter would repeat the procedure. The subject, who had earlier synchronised watches with the experimenter, would try to guess, minute by minute, which card was lying on the table. Hundreds, and sometimes thousands, of trials would be made and the results tabulated. Rhine's claims of statistically significant results were controversial, and the experiments often proved unrepeatable – repeatability of results being a benchmark of scientific validity.

Nevertheless, Rhine's groundbreaking experiments stimulated others to develop more sophisticated testing procedures, and many of the researchers he trained are still active in the field today, mainly in the United States and Britain. In the 1960s and 1970s interest focused on the psychological processes involved in PSI, with researchers attempting to uncover qualitative information about the psychological state of subjects who supposedly perform well on ESP and PK tests. They claim that subjects who believe in parapsychological phenomena tend to do better on the tests, as do subjects who are given immediate feedback after each guess. Work has also been performed on subjects in 'altered states' of consciousness, such as under hypnosis or under the influence of drugs or in a sensory-deprivation condition called the 'ganzfeld' (*see* GANZFELD STIMULATION).

Other research has focused on the phenomena of REMOTE VIEWING, the perception of distant objects clairvoyantly or by out-of-body travel. Most scientists outside the parapsychological field do not accept the existence of psychic phenomena, although some universities teach parapsychology courses and in 1985 a chair of parapsychology was established at Edinburgh University, funded in part by a bequest from the author Arthur Koestler (1905–83). Parapsychological research has often been attacked by conventional scientists as fraudulent. Rhine himself once discovered that one of his senior researchers had been faking results and dismissed him. A more serious charge is that parapsychologists are not well enough trained to be able to tell when a subject is committing a fraud against them. Parapsychologists claim that such fraud occurs only in an insignificant number of cases. Other critics have charged that in many parapsychological research projects, statistical inferences have been made, experimental design has been shoddy, and data has been misread.

A 1988 study by the National Research Council in the United States found that no scientific research conducted in the previous 130 years had proven the existence of parapsychological phenomena, although the council did find probabilistic anomalies in some experiments that could not readily be explained. Parapsychologists have countered that the study was unfair because the members of the study committee were prejudiced against parapsychology. A final criticism is that for phenomena such as extrasensory perception and psychokinesis to be true, fundamental physical laws would have to be broken. Some parapsychologists adopt the view that psychic phenomena are outside the realm of science, whereas others believe that breakthroughs in quantum physics may one day provide explanations for such phenomena.

PASSING BELL
The name given to the bell that is rung in a church when a person is near to death; it is said to have the effect of frightening away the evil spirits that are ready to take the soul as it passes from the body. In the Medieval period, bells were sometimes rung to destroy witches, as it was supposed that the sound of bells threw them off their night flight and rendered their diabolic MAGIC ineffective.

PENTAGRAM
A five-pointed star shape, used in the INVOCATION of spirits. This shape was believed to have magical properties. The spirit summoned, however potent, could not go beyond the bounds of the pentagram.

PHILOSOPHER'S STONE
The name given in ALCHEMY to a stone, powder or substance that will transmute base metals into gold.

PISCES
The twelfth sign of the ZODIAC.

dates: 19 February to 20 March.

origin and glyph: there are numerous links between the two fish and various deities from history, including Jesus Christ. The glyph represents two fish, linked, but also refers to the physical and spiritual side of the person.

ruling planet and groupings: Neptune; feminine, mutable and water.

typical traits: the Piscean person is really quite sensitive but above all is a highly sympathetic and caring person who invariably puts other people first, especially the family. They have great intuition and are good at understanding the needs of other people and make very good, kind friends. Sometimes they can take their idealistic and self-effacing stance too far, resulting in an unwillingness to face decisions, and sometimes they will rely on other, stronger, characters to lead for them. They are usually always tactful but should beware that helping others and becoming involved emotionally is not always a good thing.

family: in partnerships, Pisceans can be a little difficult to cope with, but with the right partner will help to build a welcoming home. They like visitors and to visit others, and their self-sacrificing attitude means that they will usually go a little bit further to make people happy, or an

178

occasion just right. It is important that their lack of strong will is not exploited by a stronger character.

Pisceans love children and make very good parents providing they are not too 'soft'. They do have an inner strength, and can be very tough and resourceful if the occasion demands it and when they rise to the challenge. Children often take second place to others and may need some help with their self-confidence. However, they can be very good in science and with parental encouragement can be good achievers.

business: it is not surprising, with their caring instincts, that Pisceans make good teachers and members of the health and related professions. They tend not to be particularly ambitious but can have extremely good business minds. Success is usually more likely if they have a supportive business partner. Other professions that often attract Pisceans include acting, the ministry, and anything linked with the sea.

wider aspects: Pisceans have to be careful that in helping and caring for others they tend to ignore their own pursuits or problems.

associations: *colour* – sea green; *flowers* – water lily; *gemstone* – moonstone; *trees* – willow; *food* – excesses should be avoided, salad foods are very suitable.

PK *see* PSYCHOKINESIS.

PLANCHETTE
An instrument designed for use in a SEANCE. It is a sort of mounted pencil on castors, which permits the hand to rest yet move freely to the supposed direction of the spirit control as

in automatic drawing and writing (*see* AUTOMATIC WRITING). It is said to have been invented by a French spiritualist named Planchette in 1853. *See also* OUIJA.

PLANETS

The five planets known at the time, plus the Sun and Moon, were known to the ancient world as the moving stars, and their movements were carefully checked and forecast by civilisations as remote from each other as the Chaldeans in the Middle East and the Maya in Central America. Their movement gave the planets a special significance, and they were from a very ancient time assigned correspondences with metals and colours, which related to ritual practices. For the Sun, gold and yellow; for the Moon, silver and white; for Mercury, quicksilver and grey; for Venus, copper and green; for Mars, iron and red; for Jupiter, tin and blue; for Saturn, lead and black. *See also* CELESTIAL BODIES; RULING PLANET.

POLTERGEIST

The term, compounded from the German *poltern*, 'to knock', and *geist*, 'spirit', is applied to a variety of invisible entities that manifest themselves in an unruly and disturbing manner, often involving unexplained noises, the moving or throwing of objects, vile smells or strange shrieks, as well as such curious phenomena as APPORTS. While some occurrences may appear to involve actual spirits or ghosts, the disturbances may also derive from subconscious PSYCHOKINESIS on the part of an individual. Poltergeist phenomena have been reported around the world throughout history. Before the nineteenth century, these occurrences were blamed on the DEVIL, DEMONS and witches.

In the 1930s the psychologist and psychic researcher Nandor Fodor suggested the theory that poltergeist disturbances were caused not by spirits but by individuals suffering intense repressed anger, sexual frustration and hostility. This psychological dysfunction theory has been supported by other research indicating that in a significant number of reported disturbances, the agent was a child or teenager possibly unconsciously unleashing hostility without fear of punishment. A high proportion of poltergesit activity happens when a pubescent girl is present. Psychological profiles of agents show that mental and emotional stress, personality disorders, phobias, obsessive behaviour and schizophrenia are linked to supposed poltergeist phenomena, and in some cases psychotherapy has eliminated the poltergeist disturbances.

POPPET

A CURSE DOLL, a figurine of the human form made from wax or clay and placed somewhere close to the person whom it threatens, usually with a curse inscription attached.

POSSESSION

A condition in which a person is believed to be under the control of an external force, such as a deity, DEMON or another distinct personality. Apart from possession by the Holy Spirit, Christianity regards possession as the work of the DEVIL. In Medieval theology, SATAN entered the victim directly or by using an intermediary such as a witch or wizard, causing the victim to act abominably and renounce God. According to demonological literature, sometimes the voice of the possessed person changed and sometimes even his or her appearance. The body might be thrown into convulsions, and strange objects and even creatures were said to be passed from the orifices, mainly the mouth and anus. The cure for possession by evil spirits is EXORCISM. In Judaism, the most feared and evil possession is by the Dybbuk, a doomed soul that wreaks mental and spiritual havoc on the hapless victim. In many non-Western cultures, communication with, and voluntary possession by, various deities is central to religious worship (*see* VOODOO). Similarly in Christianity, voluntary possession by the Holy Spirit is encouraged, especially in the Pentacostal movement, whose adherents may speak in tongues (*see* GLOSSOLALIA), perform faith healing and writhe uncontrollably in a form of ecstatic communion with God.

PRECOGNITION *see* ESP.

PREMONITION

A warning of an impending event, experienced as foreboding, anxiety and an intuitive sense of dread. Premonitions tend to occur before disasters, accidents and deaths. In October 1966, 28 adults and 116 children were killed in a landslide of coal waste in Aberfan, Wales. Over 200 people reported experiencing premonitions about the disaster, according to surveys taken afterwards.

In January 1967, a British Premonitions Bureau was established to collect and identify early warnings in an attempt to prevent such disasters. A similar organisation was established in New York a year later. In the following years most of the tips they were given never happened, and those that did were too inaccurate in terms of time and place to be of any help.

PRICKING

During the WITCHCRAFT craze of the sixteenth and seventeenth centuries, self-appointed WITCHFINDERS would search out suspects and prick malformations on their bodies, such as warts and birthmarks, with needles or other sharp objects. It was widely believed that witches did not feel pain when such a malformation was pricked, and it was for this reason that pricking was regarded as a reliable indication of their true nature. However, it was recognised even in the heyday of the witch hunts that many of the witchfinders were dishonest, and in his sceptical treatise on witchcraft, *The Discoverie of Witchcraft* (1584), Reginald Scot reproduces pictures of a special trick pricking knife used by some of the witchfinders, the blade of which would slide into the handle. With the aid of this trick knife the witchfinder could appear to stick the knife into the flesh of the subject and when he or she showed no sign of distress, pronounce him or her to be a witch.

PROJECTION *see* OUT-OF-BODY EXPERIENCE.

PROPHECY

A divinely inspired vision or revelation of the future, usually of important events on a grand scale. Religious prophets are men or women divinely chosen to preach the divine message, such as Jesus and Mohammed. The ancient Greeks and Romans revered ORACLES, whose pronouncements were treated as unchangeable. The ancient Hebrews had many prophets, eighteen of the thirty-nine books of the Old Testament being ascribed to prophets. In Islam, Mohammed is the Seal of the Prophets, the last of all prophets for the rest of history. Ordinary people with psychic gifts have also been called prophets. In the sixteenth century NOSTRADAMUS believed his visions were inspired by God.

PSI
The term used in PARAPSYCHOLOGY to include ESP and PSYCHOKINESIS, because both are so closely related. The term was suggested by the English psychologist Dr Robert Thouless in 1946 and is now popularly used to cover a whole range of paranormal phenomenon.

PSYCHIC
A person who can acquire information using ESP or use PSYCHOKINESIS to affect objects. Some psychics also claim to have healing abilities. Generally, psychic ability is either present from birth or triggered later in life by some traumatic physical or emotional experience.

PSYCHIC ARCHAEOLOGY
The use of psychic skills to locate dig sites and to identify artefacts. Using PSYCHOMETRY, the psychic can receive clairvoyant impressions relating to objects and photographs. DOWSING, retrocognition (seeing into the past), AUTOMATIC WRITING and REMOTE VIEWING have also been used to identify optimum dig sites and channel information from dead spirits and other entities.

Perhaps the first, best-known case of applied psychic archaeology was Frederick Bligh Bond's use of automatic writing in the excavations of the ruins of GLASTONBURY Abbey in England. Bond, an architect, was appointed by the Church of England in 1907 to find the remains of two chapels, both of which had been destroyed during the reign of Henry VIII. Bond used the services of his friend John Allen Bartlett, who was an automatic writer, and together they invoked spirits associated with the abbey to help locate the chapels' ruins. Bond received information in Latin and Old English, as well as drawings, from an entity who identified himself as 'Gulielmus Monachus', or 'William the Monk'. The monk, plus other spirits, provided details of the Edgar and Loretto Chapels. In the ensuing excavations, Bond found everything exactly as the spirits had indicated. He did not reveal the source of his success until 1917 with the publication of his book, *The Gate of Remembrance*. Angered and embarrassed, the Church of England forced Bond to resign in 1922, when excavations were stopped. Since the 1970s, psychic archaeology has been used to find dig sites in North America, Egypt, and elsewhere. Although some researchers claim high and reliable success rates with psychics, others have conducted experiments with wrapped and unwrapped artefacts that demonstrate that psychic archaeology is unreliable.

PSYCHIC CRIMINOLOGY

The use of psychics in the investigation of civil and criminal cases and in jury selection. This controversial technique has grown in the decades following World War II as a result of the publicised successes of various celebrity psychics. The primary technique is PSYCHOMETRY, the handling of objects, such as discarded weapons or the belongings of victims, and sensing their 'vibrations', which can provide information to help solve the crime. Throughout history seers and dowsers have been sought out to help locate missing persons and to solve crimes. Psychic detection was used in Europe during and after World War I.

In 1925 Sir Arthur Conan Doyle, creator of Sherlock

Holmes, predicted that the detectives of the future would be clairvoyants or would use clairvoyants. By the latter part of the twentieth century, hundreds of psychics were working regularly with police in the United States, Britain and Europe, although their success rate was erratic. Police departments remain divided over the effectiveness of psychics. Some make regular use of selected individuals and have established written procedures for doing so. Others feel psychics make no difference in solving cases. Departments that do use psychics often are reluctant to admit it publicly.

PSYCHIC READING

A session with a PSYCHIC or MEDIUM in which psychic ability is used to answer a client's questions. Most people seek psychic readings for information about the future, communication with departed loved ones, and divination for finding missing persons and objects. Such services have been rendered by psychically gifted people since ancient times. A typical reading lasts for thirty to sixty minutes. Fees vary from voluntary contributions of a nominal sum to high professional rates charged by famous psychics. The methods used in psychic readings vary, the most popular being TAROT, NUMEROLOGY, PSYCHOMETRY, PALMISTRY and CHANNELLING. Another widely used method is SCRYING, in which the psychic gazes into a crystal, a mirror or other reflective surface or into a flame.

PSYCHIC SURGERY

The alleged performing of paranormal surgery with bare hands, in which the body is opened and closed without use or benefit of surgical instruments. Patients remain fully conscious and allegedly experience no pain. While some observed surgeries remain unexplained, many have been exposed as fraud, accomplished by sleight-of-hand tricks known to most stage magicians.

Psychic surgery received much Western media attention in the 1960s and 1970s, prompting thousands of sufferers to seek treatment in the Philippines and Brazil, where psychic surgery was easily available. Some patients have reported cures that are supported by medical diagnosis, but many have not been cured. Some of the 'tumours' removed from patients have been found to be chicken or pig organs, other lumps of animal flesh or balls of cotton wool palmed by the surgeon. Kidney stones have been exposed as ordinary pebbles. Animal blood is concealed in little plastic bags in the palm or in false thumbs. In some cases the blood is already congealed when it allegedly spurts out of the patient. Using the blood, wads of cotton and sheets for diversion, the appearance of penetration can be created by folding the knuckles against the skin. Many psychic surgeons demonstrate on obese patients, whose fatty skin is easy to manipulate. If patients complain of pain, of no cure having taken place or of other postoperative problems, psychic surgeons often blame them on the spirits, on past-life karma, or on a lack of harmony between the patient and healer, and magnetic vibrations in the room.

PSYCHOKINESIS (PK)

The hypothetical influence of mind over matter without the use of any known physical or sensory means. Together with ESP, psychokinesis is investigated by PARAPSYCHOLOGY. Psychokinesis includes telekinesis, the paranormal movement of objects; LEVITATION and MATERIALISATION; mysterious events associated with given people or houses, such as RAPPINGS, overturned furniture and flying objects; and psychic healing. Since the 1930s, psychokinesis has been a major research interest among parapsychologists, especially in the United States and Russia, but, in general, the results have been inconclusive. In 1968 Russia released film and other evidence to the West showing a housewife from Leningrad, Nina Kulagina, apparently using psychokinesis to move a variety of stationary objects. She was also photographed apparently levitating objects.

In the 1970s the Israeli psychic Uri GELLER dazzled TV audiences with his alleged powers of bending metal with a few gentle strokes or taps with his fingers. Under laboratory conditions, experiments with Geller proved inconclusive, and certain professional magicians have claimed that Geller is a fraud using simple sleight-of-hand to achieve his extraordinary feats. Most scientists deny the existence of psychokinesis, and the difficulty in reproducing psychokinetic phenomena and the lack of an adequate theoretical explanation excludes it from systematic scientific investigation.

PSYCHOMETRY

A method of sensing or 'reading' from physical objects the history of each object (and the history of things and people associated with these objects) which is hidden to ordinary sensibility. The term was coined in the mid-nineteenth century by Joseph R. Buchanan, an American physiologist, who claimed it could be used to measure the 'soul' of all things. Buchanan further said that the past is entombed in the present. Researchers who followed Buchanan theorised that objects retain imprints of the past and their owners – variously called 'vibrations', 'psychic ether' and AURA – that could be picked up by sensitives. Psychometry is the main technique used in PSYCHIC CRIMINOLOGY.

PYRAMIDS
The remains of four-sided stone structures of ancient Egypt and of the pre-Columbian cultures of Central America and Mexico used as ceremonial structures and as burial chambers. In occult lore they were also used for initiation in the MYSTERIES, for calendric and astronomical purposes, and as repositories or transformers of spiritual energy. It is alleged that the polyhedral geometry of the pyramid generates supernatural powers. In 1959 a Czech radio engineer, Karl Drbal, claimed that razor blades placed in the cavity of a pyramid modelled on the dimensions of the Great Pyramid (Cheops) of Giza in Egypt would be mysteriously sharpened within twenty-four hours. Soon afterwards people were advancing the efficacy of pyramids for nurturing plants, healing wounds, curing headaches and aiding meditation.

PYTHAGORAS (*fl.* sixth century BC)
Greek philosopher and mathematician who was born on the Greek island of Samos around 570 BC and is most famous to the lay public for his famous theorem and other geometrical and mathematical achievements, Pythagoras has had a profound effect on occultism. He was sent early to Egypt and then spent ten years in Babylon, learning the arcane knowledge that both these cultures had to offer. He lived for thirty years in the Greek city of Crotona in Southern Italy, where many young men came to his philosophical school. An early

syncretist (*see* SYNCRETISM), he drew on his knowledge of the Eastern and Greek traditions and his own extraordinary facility with NUMBERS to elaborate a vision of universal harmony based on numbers. He discovered the harmonic scale in music. Pythagoras did not see the world as disorderly or a place of hidden mysteries. He believed that everything could be decoded. Like other men of exceptional intellect and impact on their generation (*see* ALBERTUS MAGNUS), a host of legends have gathered about his name. He was said to be able to call eagles down from the sky, and to have made a visit to the Underworld (a contemporary jibe said he hid in a cave).

QABBALA *see* KABBALAH.

QUADRUPLICITIES *see* GROUPINGS.

QUINTESSENCE
In occultism, this is the luminous fifth ELEMENT (invisible to ordinary sight), which was seen as binding together in union or pact the other four elements (Earth, Air, Fire, Water). *See also* GROUPINGS. In ALCHEMY the term was usually synonymous with ELIXIR.

RAPPINGS

A technical term used to describe the knocking sounds supposedly produced by spiritual entities in response to questions put to them during a SEANCE. *See* SPIRITUALISM.

RASPUTIN (1865?–1916)

A Russian mystic and prophet whose malign influence over the Russian imperial family contributed directly to the collapse of the Romanov dynasty shortly after his own death. Grigory Yefimovich Rasputin, originally surnamed Novykh, was born into a peasant family in Siberia and spent much of his youth in debauchery, receiving the name Rasputin ('debaucher'). After entering the church, however, he experienced a vision of the Virgin Mary and afterwards gained fame locally as a faith healer. Appearing at the imperial court in the Russian capital of St Petersburg about 1907, Rasputin soon acquired a reputation as a mystic and healer and became a favourite of Empress Alexandra Fyodorovna and through her influenced Tsar Nicholas II. Rasputin's hold over Alexandra stemmed from his hypnotic power to alleviate the suffering of the haemophiliac crown prince, Aleksei, and from her belief that this scruffy self-styled priest was a genuine representative of the Russian people. When Nicholas took personal command of Russian troops in 1915, Alexandra and Rasputin were virtually in charge of the government. Rasputin's licentious personal behaviour increasingly scandalised the Russian public. In 1916 a group of conservative nobles, concerned over Rasputin's pernicious political influence, plotted to assasinate him. Rasputin predicted his own death in a letter, stating that he would not live beyond 1 January 1917. He also predicted the downfall of the royal family within two years and the destruction of the aristocracy within a generation.

At the end of December 1916, Rasputin was invited to tea at the house of one of the noble conspirators and was fed cake and wine laced with cyanide. Unaffected by the poison, he was then shot several times and beaten with an iron bar. Still alive, he was dragged to the frozen River Neva, tied-up, and thrown through a hole in the ice. Within two years Tsar Nicholas and his family were dead, executed by the Bolsheviks, and within a generation, Stalinist policies had eliminated the old Russian aristocracy.

REINCARNATION

Reincarnation, the return to life in a new body after death, has a long history. In primitive shamanic belief, a dead SHA-MAN might take over the body of a young pupil, with terrific struggle and stress, and so live again. The belief in reincarnation is found in many parts of occult lore. The twentieth-century American clairvoyant Edgar Cayce went from scepticism about it to complete belief, affirming that he had once been a prince in ATLANTIS. Another occultist, Rudolf STEINER, elaborated a whole series of future incarnations awaiting humanity.

REMOTE VIEWING
Seeing or sensing remote objects clairvoyantly, using an 'inner eye' or allegedly through OUT-OF-BODY travel. It is a skill claimed by shamans in Tibet, Siberia, Africa and India for centuries. In the eighteenth century, Emanuel SWEDENBORG was renowned for his remote visions. In the eighteenth and early nineteenth centuries, mesmerists discovered that many of their hypnotised subjects could give detailed accounts of distant locations or could 'see' into other people's bodies or brains (*see* MESMER, HYPNOSIS). In the late nineteenth century psychic investigators of the Society of Psychical Research in London conducted many experiments into 'travelling clairvoyance' with subjects who closed their eyes, were blindfolded or even blind.

In the 1970s, two American physicists, Russell Targ and Harold Puthoff, established a project at Stanford University to exploit data amassed by previous research and to conduct further experiments into the phenomena. They concluded that remote viewing occurred naturally in many people's lives and that it was possible to train people as remote viewers, regardless of innate psychic abilities. Subjects could be taught to 'visit' a location and accurately describe buildings, people and natural features. Intelligence agencies, such as the CIA and KGB, are now known to have used remote viewers to help penetrate the Iron Curtain during the Cold War.

RETROCOGNITION *see* ESP.

ROSICRUCIANS

The Order of the Rosy Cross, or Rosicrucians, is a world-wide esoteric society whose official emblem combines a rose and a cross. The society was apparently founded in Europe in Medieval times and was given impetus by the publication of three anonymous pamphlets in successive years: *Fama Fraternitatis* (*Account of the Brotherhood*, 1614), the *Confessio Fraternitatis* (*Confession of the Brotherhood*, 1615) and *The Third Chemical Wedding of Christian Rosencreutz* (1616). They describe the initiation into the spiritual and alchemical mysteries of the East (particularly of ancient Egypt) of Christian Rosenkreuz, who was allegedly born in 1378 but is presumed to be an allegorical figure.

The expressed purpose of the *Fama* and associated writings was the spiritualisation of individuals according to quasi-Christian and esoteric principles. Scholars believe these pamphlets, which are anti-papal and promote Protestant ethics, were probably written by the German Lutheran pastor Johan Valentin Andreae (1586–1654). Despite arousing enthusiasm in the expanding occult community, no later records exist for membership of the Order.

In the eighteenth century various tracts and manifestoes were published asserting the existence of the Brothers of the Rosy Cross, and several groups claiming Rosicrucian origins were active in Russia, Poland and Germany. The first Rosicrucian society in the United States was founded in Pennsylvania in 1694. In 1909 Harvey Spencer Lewis founded The Ancient Mystical Order Rosae Crucis (AMORC), which now has its headquarters in San Jose, California. Lewis claimed to have been initiated into the Brotherhood in France. The AMORC is an international fraternal order that operates through a system of lodges and fosters the Rosicrucian philosophy of developing humankind's highest potentialities and psychic powers. Through study and practice, members strive for perfection, with the ultimate goal being admittance into the Lodge and the attainment of true knowledge, or cosmic consciousness. Students progress through twelve degrees of mastery, with the tenth through twelfth degrees conferred psychically, usually in the Order's temples in the East. As in THEOSOPHY, such perfection comes only after various reincarnations, each devoted to achieving a greater oneness with the Supreme Being. Rosicrucians claim influence on FREEMASONRY, especially since the eighteenth Masonic degree is the Sovereign Prince Rose Croix of Heredom.

RULING PLANET

In astrology, the PLANET that is predominant for each sign of the ZODIAC, that is, the planet that appears in the ecliptic (the annual path that the Sun apparently forms in the heavens) at the time of the sign. Each planet rules one sign, except Venus and Mercury, which each rule two.

There are additional features and weightings given to the rulings, known as exaltation, detriment and fall. Each planet is exalted when it is in a particular sign from which it works well and with which there is a notable similarity, resulting in more significance being attributed to it in an interpretation. Each planet also has a sign of detriment, when the planet is said to be debilitated. The sign opposite to exaltation is called the fall sign. This is when the planet is thought to be weak.

Planet	Ruling in	Exalted in	Detrimental	Fall
Sun	Leo	Aries	Aquarius	Libra
Moon	Cancer	Taurus	Capricorn	Scorpio
Mercury	Gemini and Virgo	Virgo	Sagittarius	Pisces
Venus	Taurus and Libra	Pisces	Aries	Virgo
Mars	Aries	Capricorn	Libra	Cancer
Jupiter	Sagittarius	Cancer	Gemini	Capricorn
Saturn	Capricorn	Libra	Cancer	Aries
Uranus	Aquarius	Scorpio	Leo	Taurus
Neptune	Pisces	Leo	Virgo	Aquarius
Pluto	Scorpio	Virgo	Taurus	Pisces

Before William Herschel discovered Uranus in 1781, there were only seven planets (including the Sun and Moon) and therefore three further planets ruled two signs: Saturn ruled Aquarius as well as Capricorn, Jupiter ruled Pisces as well as Sagittarius, and Mars ruled Scorpio as well as Aries.

RUNES

An ancient Norse and Germanic alphabet, to the symbols of which were ascribed magical properties and which were used mainly for charms and inscriptions on stone, wood, metal or bone. In legend, the runes come from the Volsung, a Nordic people who were the guardians of the forests as they grew again after the last Ice Age. Perhaps derived ultimately from the Etruscan alphabet, the runic alphabet was spread throughout Europe, Russia and Britain by Viking invaders and travellers, from Norway to Constantinople, and rune usage was at its height during the Dark Ages.

There were several different systems of runes. In Britain the earliest alphabet had twenty-four letters divided into three groups of eight. The groups were named after Norse deities: Freya, Hagal and Tiu. Runes were carved on stone, bone or wood and were cast in a form of DIVINATION.

The use of runes had died out by the fifteenth century as the Roman Catholic Church eclipsed paganism. In the late nineteenth century German occultists revived interest in runes, which became associated with Teutonic racial superiority. The Nazi SWASTIKA is the runic symbol for Thor's hammer and also a symbol of the Earth Mother, and the runic S symbol was used by the SS, the Nazi secret police. *See also* FUTHARC; NINE WORLDS OF CREATION.

S

SABBAT *or* WITCHES' SABBATH

The Witches' Sabbath was supposed to be a weekly mid-night convention of witches, warlocks and DEMONS, a combination of cannibalistic feast, sexual orgy and blasphemous SATAN worship. It was believed that Lucifer appeared in the form of a black goat to preside over the hellish proceedings and coupled with all or some of those present. According to witchcraft confessions (most extracted by torture), the Sabbat started with the lighting of a fire from which the witches lit torches or black candles. Lucifer would then appear, and one by one the participants would make some form of obeisance to their master. Usually this took the form of the *osculum obscenum*, kissing the Devil's anus. The central feature of the Sabbat was always a feast followed by an indiscriminate sexual orgy between demons and witches, witches and warlocks and warlocks and demons. The pleasure in these occasions cannot have been high, however. In confessions the food and wine are often described as vile smelling and tasting, and sex with demons icy and painful. If such occasions ever took place, it was only as elaborate fantasies in the minds of the theologians, demonologists and WITCHHUNTERS themselves.

SACRED SPEAR
The spear of LONGINUS, which pierced the side of Christ, also known as the Spear of Destiny.

SAGITTARIUS
The ninth sign of the ZODIAC.

dates: 23 November to 21 December.

origin and glyph: the origin is unknown, but the glyph, represents the arrow of the Centaur.

ruling planet and groupings: Jupiter, masculine, mutable and fire.

typical traits: Sagittarians are essentially gregarious, friendly and enthusiastic, with a desire to achieve all goals that are set. They are rarely beset by depression, but their inborn enthusiasm can sometimes take them too far, and they may take risks. Although they are versatile and intelligent, their desire to jump from the task in hand to the next may result in some tasks being unfinished. In excess, their good qualities can become a nuisance, leading to tactless, hurtful comments (without the intent to hurt) and jokes that go too far.

family: freedom is important to Sagittarians, so much so that it may inhibit long-term relationships. After settling down, however, they are good in the family context, and their enthusiasm can help lift boredom. They enjoy a friendship or partnership more if they are given a loose rein to enable them to do what they want.

Often their ultimate goal is not materialistic but more spiritual.

As parents, this approach to life means that they encourage their children to be outgoing, and this is fine providing a child is not nervous or shy. The natural enthusiasm of Sagittarian children should be guided to productive ends, and their instinctive dislike of rules should be dealt with diplomatically. There is considerable potential in the child who has a gentle guiding hand upon him or her.

business: Sagittarians are not interested primarily in material gain and because they are particularly interested in education and travel, that is where money may be spent. Work of a varied nature is preferred, but care should be taken to make sure details are not omitted in the race to move on to something new. There is a natural desire to help others, which may manifest itself in a career in teaching, counselling, lecturing, the Church, law, and publishing.

wider aspects: when both mind and body have a certain degree of freedom, Sagittarians are at their best and will then employ their versatility and intellectual strengths to the full.

associations: *colour* – purple, deep blue; *flowers* – carnations; *gemstone* – topaz; *trees* – oak, ash, and birch; *food* – good food is enjoyed but overindulgence should be avoided. Specifically currants and the onion family.

SATAN

In the Judeo-Christian tradition, Satan, from the Hebrew word for 'adversary', is the personification of evil and all that is hostile to God and his will. In the Septuagint (Greek translation of the Hebrew Bible) the translation of 'satan' is given as 'diabolos' meaning 'devil'. Both terms are usually employed synonymously. In the Old Testament Satan is presented as a distinct personality of darkness and accusation, a type of heavenly prosecutor. In the New Testament, he is described as the one who has the power of death, rules with lies and deception, accuses humankind before God, and opposes the purpose of God in the world. In later Christian tradition Satan was described as a fallen angel, and Christianity has always regarded Hell, the region of fiery torment below the earth, as Satan's realm. Many other cultures outside the Hebrew tradition have a concept of a leader of the powers of darkness. The Babylonians, Chaldeans and Persians believed in a dualism between the forces of darkness and light. Ahriman, in Zoroastrianism, and Seth, the god of evil in Egyptian mythology, and 'Mara' in Buddhism manifest characteristics similar to Satan's.

SATANISM

The worship of SATAN. It involves BLACK MAGIC, sorcery and the INVOCATION of DEMONS and the forces of darkness, who are propitiated by blood sacrifices and similar rites. In Christian cultures these ceremonies include the BLACK MASS, a mockery of the Christian rite. Medieval Christian writers tended to label any dualist sect (such as the Bogomils and Albigensians) as Satanist. From the later Middle Ages, Satanism and WITCHCRAFT were considered as synonymous. There was a Satanist revival in the late nineteenth century, and evidence exists that the cult persists. Satanists, or Luciferians, believe that Satan is the power behind the processes of nature. What is natural is acceptable. Sin is only what is unpleasant. Unlike the Christian God – stern and moralistic, repressive and chastening – Satan is the leader of a liberated people who are free and actually encouraged to indulge in the good things of life, including uninhibited sexual activity.

SCORPIO

The eighth sign of the ZODIAC.

dates: 24 October to 22 November.

origin and glyph: the origin of the scorpion is unknown, although it appears in numerous guises in ancient history. The glyph symbolises a serpent's coil and is linked with the male genitalia.

ruling planet and groupings: Pluto; feminine, fixed and water.

typical traits: Scorpians can show rather a mix of behaviour and character, on the one hand being very determined and strong-willed, and on the other being obsessive, awkward and arrogant. Once committed to something, whether a person or an ideal, they will be very faithful, although they are susceptible to being melodramatic, and when emotions become involved logic suffers. They are usually energetic, wanting the most out of life, whether at work or play, and will not relinquish their goal easily. Although they are perfectly capable of sacrificing others, they do hold on to what is right and will exhibit a strong sense of fair play and reason.

family: the Scorpian's desire to stay with a relationship holds good for partnerships, although their energy may need to be channelled if it is not to prove disruptive. They prefer people who are equally strong-willed but, despite outward appearances, may themselves be weaker than they look. They are certainly prone to depression, from which they find it hard to emerge, and this may contribute to the apparent extremes in marriage – some are very good, others less so.

As parents they will do their utmost for their offspring, but they can push a little too much and should consciously develop a balanced approach to parenthood, allowing their children some freedom.

Some children are often very affectionate but equally prone to sudden tempers. They should be helped to talk over problems to avoid depressed silences, and their emotional energies should be diverted into productive occupations.

business: when running a business, a Scorpian will work to his or her very limit to help ensure success and, to a certain extent, they welcome challenges and problems. They can employ charm when necessary but can also be hard and demanding at times. They also like financial security and are willing to work for it. Scorpians are well suited to being in the medical profession or in a profession where analysis and research are required.

wider aspects: the character of a Scorpian is built up of a fine balance of attributes, which, in a positive sense, can yield a tremendous achiever but conversely may produce someone riven with jealousy.

associations: *colour* – deep red; *flowers* – dark red flowers such as geraniums; *gemstone* – opal; *trees* – thorn-bearing varieties; *food* – foods with strong flavours.

SCOT *or* **SCOTT, MICHAEL** (*c*.1175–*c*.1230)
A famous Medieval Scottish scholar-wizard-astrologer, tutor in astrology to the Emperor Frederick II and author of astrological works. His legendary encounters with the DEVIL have left their mark on the landscape of Scotland in numerous places, including the Eildon Hills.

SCOT *or* **SCOTT, REGINALD** (*c*.1538–1599)
English writer, member of parliament and country gentleman who spent most of his life in Kent. He wrote two books, the first treatise on hop-growing, published in 1574, and *Discoverie of Witchcraft*, published in 1584. This drew on the works of Greek and Arabic writers as well as Europeans, and Scot also included the superstitions respecting WITCHCRAFT that he had observed in courts of law in country districts where the prosecution of witches was increasing and in village life where the belief in witchcraft flourished in a variety of forms. With an insight that was far in advance of his times, he set out to prove that the belief in witchcraft and magic was rejected by both reason and religion and that spiritualistic manifestations were illusions conjured up by mental disturbances in the observers. He wrote with the philanthropic aim of stopping the cruel persecution that generally pursued the poor, the aged and the simple who were the people most likely to be accused of being witches. He laid the blame for the maintenance of the belief in witchcraft at the door of the Roman Catholic Church. While he attacked the writings of credulous writers like Jean Bodin (1530–96), author of *Démonie des Sorciers* (1580) and Jacobus Sprenger, joint author of MALLEUS MALEFICARUM (1494), he respected the views of others, like Cornelius AGRIPPA.

Scot's *Discoverie* was an exhaustive encyclopedia of contemporary beliefs about witchcraft, spirits, alchemy, magic and sleight-of-hand. He was a victim to contemporary superstition only in his references to medicine and astrology. He believed in the medicinal value of the unicorn's horn and thought that precious stones owed their origin to the influence of the heavenly bodies. Scot's book attracted widespread attention and for a time was influential on magistrates and members of the clergy, but the ancient belief in witches was not easily uprooted and many writers came to its rescue.

Following attacks by others on *Discoverie*, James VI of Scotland repeated the attempt in his *Daemonologie* (1597), in which he described Scot's opinions as 'damnable'. On his accession to the English throne, James went a step further and ordered all copies of *Discoverie* to be burnt. Shakespeare drew on Scot's book hints for his picture of the witches in *Macbeth*, and Thomas Middleton drew on it for his play *Witch*.

SCRYING

A method of DIVINATION using a crystal ball, shiny stone, MIRROR or other reflective object or surface until clairvoyant visions appear. The art dates back to the ancient Egyptians and Arabs, and practitioners aim to answer questions, solve problems, find lost objects or people and help solve crimes. The tool of scryers is called a speculum, which can be any object but is usually one with a reflective surface.

The French physician and astrologer NOSTRADAMUS used a brass bowl of water on a tripod. Dr John DEE, astrologer to Queen Elizabeth I, used a crystal egg and a black obsidian mirror. The stereotypical speculum is the crystal ball as popularised by gypsy fortune-tellers.

SEAL OF SOLOMON

An occult symbol, often found as a TALISMAN or AMULET, formed of two regular interlocking triangles, making a six-pointed star and denoting the four ELEMENTS.

SEANCE

A gathering of people for the purpose of investigating or ex-periencing supernormal or psychic phenomena. In the past they were sometimes called 'circles', because participants, called 'sitters', sat around a table (or on chairs arranged in a circle) in order to link hands, in the belief that this boosted the psychic forces that encourage paranormal manifestations. Generally seances involve a medium who enters a trance-like state and contacts a 'spirit friend' or 'spirit helper'. The spirit then communicates with the gathering through the medium, either mentally or directly, using the medium's vo-cal chords. In the nineteenth century, seances were domi-nated by physical manifestations, such as RAPPINGS, strange smells, LEVITATION and MATERIALISATION, most episodes of which were eventually exposed as having been fraudulent. Because of these fraudulent associations, the term 'seance' has fallen into disuse and modern psychic researchers and mediums use the term 'sitting'.

SECOND SIGHT

The power of seeing things future or distant, particularly in the Scottish Highlands. Some of the Scottish 'seers' declared this power to be hereditary while others maintained that it could be imparted by teaching.

SECRET COMMONWEALTH, THE

The title of a book which was published in 1691 by the Rev. Robert Kirk in which he describes in great detail the world of the fairies as revealed to him by the fairies who lived in the hill, anciently known as Dun Shee (Gaelic: 'fairy hill'), in his own parish in the southern Highlands of Scotland.

SHAKESPEARE, WILLIAM (1564–1616)

The frequency of occult events in Shakespeare's plays can be put down to the intense interest that such matters had for enquiring Tudor minds of which his was merely one of the most brilliant. The Renaissance was revealing much of old pagan lore at this time, whilst Medieval attitudes and practices were still commonplace throughout the countryside. The witches of *Macbeth*, the ghost in *Hamlet*, the woodland fairies of *A Midsummer Night's Dream*, all were things that even Shakespeare's sophisticated London and court audiences could still half-believe in. The thoughts and vocabulary of occultism were obviously familiar to Shakespeare, but just as they would have been to any interested man of the world. *See also* SCOT, REGINALD.

SHAMANS AND SHAMANISM

The word *shaman* comes from Siberia, and its origins lie in words meaning 'to become excited'. Shamans were perhaps the first people to seek to penetrate and interpret the secret currents of life. The essence of shamanism was to be able to enter a state of trance in which this communion with natural powers could be experienced. It is a magical vocation (*see* OCCULT POWERS) but also requires long and arduous preparation. In past times, shamans would put themselves to great physical suffering in order to steel and accustom their bodies to a wide range of experiences. In the trance state they might walk through a fire or on pointed sticks; they had to be impervious to pain, heat and cold. Drumming and dancing were the methods of achieving the trance-state. In trance, the shaman's spirit left his body and travelled to lower or upper worlds to meet godlike beings from whom he would receive knowledge. It might be the knowledge of who had committed an offence, or of where deer might be found, or of whether the tribe should move or stay. There is much about basic shamanism that is primitive and ignorant, inevitably so as it is so ancient a tradition. But it has become of great interest in recent times, partly through SYN-CRETISM and partly through the feeling that its simplicity of approach, its closeness to nature, has much to teach the complex modern mind.

SHROUD OF TURIN

An ancient strip of linen bearing bloodstains and the brownish image of a bearded man, which was believed by many people to be the actual burial cloth of Jesus Christ. The shroud, 4.34 metres (14 feet 3 inches) long and 1.09 metres (3 feet 7 inches) wide, can be traced through documentation back to 1354, but its history before that date is obscure. Since 1578 it has been preserved and venerated in St John's Cathedral in Turin. Photographed for the first time in 1898, the image on the shroud – of the front and back of a crucified man about two metres (six feet tall) – was revealed to be negative rather than positive. Details of the Biblical account of Christ's burial – specifically the anointing of the body – conflict with the natural possibility of an imprint such as that on the Shroud of Turin, and Vatican-sponsored carbon-dating tests conducted in 1988 indicated that the shroud itself dates no earlier than 1260.

SIBYL *see* ORACLE.

SIMON MAGUS
A magician of Samaria in the first century AD. He became famous for his sorceries but was converted to Christianity by Saint Philip, although later he tried to purchase the power of the Holy Spirit from the Apostles Peter and John.

SITTING *see* SEANCE.

SPEAKING IN TONGUES *see* GLOSSOLALIA.

SPIRITUALISM
A system of religious beliefs centred on the assumption that communication with the dead, or spirits, is possible. Spiritualism as a movement began in the United States in 1848 with the activities of Margaret Fox and, to a lesser extent, her two sisters, of Hydesville, New York. The Fox sisters were able to produce spirit RAPPINGS in answer to questions put to them. After moving to Rochester, New York State, and receiving a wider audience through a series of increasingly elaborate public seances, their fame spread to both sides of the Atlantic. By the mid-1850s they had inspired a host of imitators, and spiritualism claimed two million followers. Margaret Fox admitted later in life that she had produced rapping noises through manipulation of her joints.

The repertoire of the early mediums included table LEVITATIONS, ESP, speaking in a spirit's voice during trances,

AUTOMATIC WRITING, and the manifestation of APPARITIONS and ECTOPLASM. All such phenomena were attributed by the mediums to the agency of spirits. Early supporters of spiritualistic phenomena included the American journalist Horace Greeley (1811–72) and the British author Sir Arthur Conan DOYLE. Support for spiritualism diminished, however, as many nineteenth-century mediums proved to be fakes.

Spiritualism has had, since its inception, a large following. Many churches and societies have been founded that profess some variety of spiritualistic beliefs. It achieved particularly widespread popular appeal during the 1850s and 1860s and immediately following World War I. Closely aligned with other NEW AGE beliefs, belief in spiritualism again became popular during the 1980s, particularly in the United States. One new facet of spiritualism is that modern-day channellers or mediums are as apt to attempt contact with extraterrestrials or spirits from ancient mythical societies as they are to try to communicate with the recently deceased.

STEINER, RUDOLF (1861–1925)

Austrian philosopher, scientist, artist and educator who was the originator of the social philosophy called anthro-posophy. A Christianised version of THEOSOPHY, this doctrine asserts that humans possess a faculty of spiritual cognition, or pure thought, that functions independently of the senses. Anthroposophy strives for the most effective development of this faculty. Steiner founded the Anthroposophical Society in 1912, and it now has branches throughout the world and is especially popular in Britain. He travelled extensively in Europe, lecturing on spiritual science, the arts, social sciences, religion, education, agriculture and health. Over 350 of his works have been published, including collections of lectures, books, articles, reviews and dramas. His occult philosophy is outlined in key titles such as *Knowledge of the Higher Worlds and Its Attainment* (1904–5), and *An Outline of Occult Science* (1909). His teachings inspired the development of the Waldorf School movement and of schools for handicapped or maladjusted children. His agricultural methods for preparing soil inspired chemical-free organic farming and gardening. He created eurythmy (expressive movement to music and speech), and his guidelines on holistic medicine and pharmacology are still widely respected. *See also* ATLANTIS; LEMURIA.

STIGMATA

Bleeding marks resembling the wounds suffered by Jesus Christ when he was crucified. They are manifested on the hands, on the feet, near the heart, and on the head and shoulders. The stigmata are not usual bodily lacerations (the blood appears to discharge through the unbroken skin), do not deteriorate in the usual fashion of wounds and are not susceptible to medical treatment. Francis of Assisi (later Saint Francis) was the first and best-known stigmatic. In September 1224 he reportedly began to bleed from his palms and feet after meditating on the crucifixion of Christ.

More than 330 cases are known of Christians who have been stigmatised. Stigmatics are deeply pious, and the stigmata often appear after lengthy meditations on the crucifixion or contemplation of a sacred image or object. Bleeding is also likely to occur during the traditional times of commemoration of Christ's passion – Fridays, Lent, and especially Good Friday. In many cases stigmatisation can be explained by natural causes such as the physical and psychic conditions of the person, along with a strong interest in and devotion to the sufferings of Christ. In a number of cases, however, stigmatisation has been accepted by the Roman Catholic Church as attributable only to supernatural causes; sixty stigmatics whose lives have been marked by great holiness and mystical experiences have been either canonised or beatified.

STONEHENGE

The most famous prehistoric megalith (standing-stone monument) in Europe, located thirteen kilometres (eight miles) north of Salisbury in Wiltshire, England. Excavations and radiocarbon dating have revealed that Stonehenge had an exceptionally long history of use as a ceremonial or religious centre or both.

It was constructed in three major phases over the period from around 3500 BC to 1100 BC. It originally began as a circular ditch including a bank with a ring of fifty-six burial pits – named 'Aubrey holes' for their seventeenth-century discoverer, John Aubrey (1626–97). Around 2100 BC, a double circle of bluestone menhirs (large, rough-hewn standing stones), thought to have come from the Preseli Mountains of southwestern Wales, was erected within the earlier ring. In the final stage of construction, from around 2000 BC, a circle of about thirty upright stones (made from local sandstone called 'sarsen') were set up, their tops linked by lintel stones to form a continuous circle about thirty metres (one hundred feet) across. At a later date, around 1550 BC, the bluestones were finally rearranged in the circle and horseshoe shape whose remains survive today.

Stonehenge is unique because of its long period of use and the precision of its plan and its architectural details. The traditional thesis that Stonehenge was a DRUID temple is untenable, because the Druids did not appear in Britain until a few hundred years before the Christian era. In recent years many attempts have been made to interpret Stonehenge as a prehistoric astronomical observatory or some form of solar temple, but the site is now so ruined, and so much restored, that any attempt to ascertain its original alignments must rely principally on guesswork. All that can be said with confidence is that from around 2000 BC onwards the structure's axis of symmetry pointed roughly in the direction of the sunrise at the summer solstice.

SUCCUBUS *see* INCUBUS.

SUMMERS, MONTAGUE (1880–1948)
Author of two important studies of witchcraft, *The History of Witchcraft and Demonology*, and *The Geography of Witchcraft*. Summers was a trained priest, but his approach is narrative and anecdotal, over-credulous rather than arbitrarily dismissive.

SWASTIKA
An ancient symbol of good fortune. The word has Sanskrit roots, meaning 'good luck', and it is a symbol found in a number of Indo-European cultures. Originally a Sun symbol, it became the sign of Thor's hammer in the RUNIC alphabet. In German it was known as the *Hakenkreuz*, or crooked cross. Its Nordic association made it of interest to the likes of the THULE SOCIETY, who introduced it to the Nazi move-

ment. But its position was reversed, so that its direction, instead of being clockwise, was anti-clockwise – the direction of unreason and chaos.

SWEDENBORG, EMANUEL (1688–1772)

Swedish scientist, theosophist and mystic, a pioneer in both scientific, religious and spiritual thought. For most of his life Swedenborg pursued a conventional, albeit brilliant, career. Educated at Uppsala University, he first became a natural scientist and official with the Swedish Royal College of Mines (1710–45), concentrating on research and theory. His foremost scientific writing is *Opera Philosophica et Mineralia* (*Philosophical and Mineralogical Works*), (three volumes, 1734), a unique combination of metaphysics, cosmology and science.

A first-rate scientific theorist and inventor, Swedenborg, in some of his insights, anticipated scientific progress by more than a century. Visited by a mystic illumination in 1745, Swedenborg claimed a direct vision of a spiritual world underlying the natural sphere. He began having dreams, ecstatic visions, trances and mystical illusions in which he communicated with Jesus Christ and God and was granted a view of the order of the universe that was radically different from the teachings of the Christian church. He resigned his job to concentrate full-time on his ecstatic visions and to transcribe the knowledge imparted to him from the spiritual world. His voluminous works from this period are presented as divinely revealed Biblical interpretations. In his system, best reflected in *Divine Love and Wisdom* (1763), Swedenborg conceived of three spheres: divine mind, spiritual world and natural world. Each corresponds to a degree of being in God and in humankind: love, wisdom and use (end, cause and effect). Through devotion to each degree, unification with it takes place and a person obtains his or her destiny, which is union with creator and creation.

Unlike many mystics, Swedenborg proposed an approach to spiritual reality and God through, rather than in rejection of, material nature. His twelve-volume compendium *The Heavenly Arcana* (1747–56) represents a unique synthesis between modern science and religion. In response to a vision of the 'last judgment' and the 'return of Christ', Swedenborg proclaimed the advent of the New Church, an idea that found social expression in the Swedenborgian Societies and in the foundation of the Church of the New Jerusalem in England in 1778 and in the United States in 1792. Many of his views were adopted by nineteenth-century SPIRITUALISM, and many of his ideas were also disseminated in the works of writers and poets such as William Blake, Samuel Taylor Coleridge and Henry James.

SYLPH
The spirit beings associated with the ELEMENT of Air, usually represented as small, semi-translucent winged creatures.

SYMPATHETIC MAGIC *see* MAGIC.

SYNCRETISM
The process by which systems of belief, which once were separate and which arise from different sources, begin to blend and to take elements from one another. This is particularly marked in modern occultism, although it has always been a feature, since practitioners have always been interested in what they could discern about other teachings. The

development of mass global travel and of electronic media has accentuated this trend to the point where many occult processes are combined. The same person may use the TAROT and the American Indian medicine wheel or combine Kabbalistic and Tibetan means of DIVINATION. This potentially confusing procedure is justified by the underlying resemblances of all occult studies. They share the same intention, which is of seeking harmony with the invisible and not fully understood forces that rule the cosmos.

TALISMAN

Specially prepared objects – of stone, metal, wood, parchment and so on – inscribed with magical signs, characters or drawings. Once endowed with magical properties, the object is believed to bring the owner good luck, success, health and virility. The power of a talisman can derive from nature, directly from God, or from a magical ritual, such as those described in the GRIMOIRES, textbooks of ceremonial magic. *See* AMULET.

TAROT

A deck of playing cards used for DIVINATION and fortune-telling. The tarot was brought from the East to Italy in the fourteenth century by gypsies or returning Crusaders. The origin of the cards is obscure, and theories that the tarot is based on the Hebrew alphabet or on Egyptian or Hindu mythology have not been conclusively proved. It seems likely that it first began as a card game and gained further significance later, and it is still the basis of a game, *les tarots* in French, *tarocchi* ('trumps') in Italian, played in France and Italy. In 1781 a French Occultist, Antoine Court de Gebelin, linked the tarot pack to what he called 'the Book of THOTH', the divine Egyptian founder of all magic.

In the nineteenth century the occultist Eliphas LEVI further linked the tarot pack to the KABBALAH, finding many symmetries, although there is nothing in the Kabbalah that corresponds to tarot cards. These ideas were taken up by some of the members of the ORDER OF THE GOLDEN DAWN, notably Arthur Edward Waite and Aleister CROWLEY, and their work has given us the divinatory tarot pack still in very widespread use today.

The tarot deck consists of seventy-eight cards, which are divided into two groups. The Minor, or Lesser, Arcana, the precursor of the modern deck, is made up of fifty-six cards divided into four suits. The wands suit corresponds to the modern clubs suit; cups to hearts; swords to spades; and pentacles to diamonds. Each suit has fourteen cards, with numbered cards from ace to ten and four unnumbered face cards: king, queen, knight and knave. (The four knight cards have been eliminated in the modern deck.) The Major, or Greater, Arcana consists of twenty-two cards, each bearing a title and a picture, such as the Hanged Man, the Wheel of Fortune, Judgment, and the Moon, rich in occult and astrological symbolism. Twenty-one of the cards are numbered. The twenty-second card, the Fool, numbered 0, is analogous to the modern joker.

In fortune-telling, either the full pack or the Major Arcana alone is used. The relationship of one card to another, as laid out in a number of different configurations, is as important as the significance of each individual card. As can be seen, the tarot is not a fixed system. New variants are always being brought forward, seeking to make the tarot relevant to cultures where it was not previously known, like that of the American Indians. It is very much an evolving tradition.

TAURUS

The second sign of the ZODIAC.

dates: 21 April to 21 May.

origin and glyph: the bull's head, which has links with early civilisations in Egypt.

ruling planet and groupings: Venus; feminine, fixed and earth.

typical traits: Taureans rely upon stability and security, both in an emotional and financial context, but granted this they can be extremely reliable, patient and tenacious. They tend to be persistent, methodical and see things through to the end, and this can be reflected in their steady progress through life, including their career. Their lack of flexibility can often lead to resistance to change, even when it is for the better. However, when facing the challenge, they usually cope better than most. Taureans are practical people who dislike waste, and they tend to have high standards.

family: a good partnership is important to Taureans, and this means a happy harmonious partnership. Their need to put down roots and build can render them very good at making a home, as does the practical side of their character. They usually make good husbands and wives, and parents, but they may make the mistake of getting stuck in a rut. One of the faults of Taureans is jealousy and possessiveness, which can often be applied to a partner.

Having established a good home, Taureans will probably consider children to be very important, and the parents will strive to make their children happy. Babies and toddlers can be slow to reach the obvious milestones such as walking, but in later childhood things need to be learnt only once. Discipline is important because Taureans are essentially traditional and look for rules and guidance.

business: although Taureans do not like taking risks, they are ambitious. However, they are more likely to stay with a job than to chop and change, and will quite possibly remain in uninteresting employment because the income is well nigh guaranteed. Sure handling of money and financial affairs comes easily to Taureans, and many find careers in the financial sector.

wider aspects: routine is vital, and change or uncertainty makes them uncomfortable. They enjoy leisure pursuits but must guard against becoming too lazy.

associations: *colour* – pale shades, especially blue, pink and green; *flowers* – rose, poppy and foxglove; *gemstone* – emerald; *trees* – apple, pear, ash; *food* – generally like their food.

TELEPATHY

The transfer of thoughts, images and sensations between minds without conventional verbal, written or physical means of communication. Although not scientifically proven, the phenomenon has been described, and often accepted as normal, in many cultures and societies throughout history. It was the first psychic phenomenon to be studied by members of the newly created Society for Psychic Research, established in London in 1884. More recent research indicates that telepathy often occurs spontaneously during crises, when an individual at a distance is in danger. Information may be transferred as fragmentary images, dreams, visions or words that suddenly pop into the mind. It is more common among women than men, perhaps because telepathy is closely tied to the emotions. No satisfactory theory has yet been advanced to explain the phenomenon.

TEMPLARS *see* ORDER OF THE KNIGHTS TEMPLAR.

TETRAGRAMMATON *see* KABBALAH.

TEUTONIC KNIGHTS
A German order of chivalry, which was formed at the time of the Crusades. Its aim was to spread Christianity into the still pagan lands to the east of Prussia. The order was open only to those of noble birth, and for centuries it exercised great power in what are now eastern Germany and Poland. Their badge was the Jerusalem Cross, or cross-potent (with an additional cross-piece at the end of each arm). Much semi-mystical legend has grown up around the order, which was abolished by Napoleon in 1809, and in a perverted manner its forms and supposed rituals were re-enacted by Nazi leaders such as Heinrich Himmler.

THEOSOPHY
A term derived from the Greek *theos* ('god') and *sophia* ('wisdom'), which means wisdom of or about God. In a general sense, theosophy refers to a broad spectrum of occult or mystical philosophies, often pantheistic in nature. The Western theosophical tradition may be said to be derived from the

HERMETIC tradition of the Renaissance and post-Renaissance and is characterised by an emphasis on the hidden tradition passed down in a succession from the ancients. This tradition is thought to provide a key to nature and to humanity's place in the universe. More specifically, the term refers to the Theosophical Society, its offshoots, and the doctrines held by its members.

The most important early figure in the movement was Helena Petrovna BLAVATSKY, who, along with Colonel Henry Steel Olcott (1832–1907) and William Q. Judge (1851–96), founded the society in New York City in 1875. In numerous works, including *Isis Unveiled* (1877) and *The Secret Doctrine* (1888), Blavatsky elaborated an amalgamation of previous theories that were claimed to be derived from the MAHATMAS of ancient India. The Theosophical Society grew rapidly in Europe and the United States, its two most influential adherents being Annie BESANT and Rudolf STEINER.

According to Madame Blavatsky, the doctrines of theosophy rest on three fundamental propositions. The first postulates an omnipresent, boundless and immutable principle that transcends human understanding. It is the one unchanging reality, or infinite potentiality, inherent in all life and covers all that humans have tried to say about God. The second deals with the universality of the law of periodicity recorded by science as found in all nature. As morning, noon and night are succeeded by morning again, so birth, youth, adulthood and death are succeeded by rebirth. Reincarnation is the process of human development, in which all growth is governed by the law of justice or KARMA. The third proposition declares the fundamental identity of all souls with the universal Over-Soul, suggesting that brotherhood is a fact in nature and the obligatory pilgrimage for every soul through numerous cycles of incarnation. Theosophy admits of no privileges or special gifts in humans except those won by effort and merit. Perfected individuals and great teachers, such as Buddha, Jesus and the mahatmas, are universal beings, the flower of evolution.

After the death of Madame Blavatsky in 1891, a battle for leadership of the society ensued, from which Annie Besant emerged as leader in Europe and Asia, whereas William Judge led a secessionist movement in the United States. Under Besant, the society flourished. In 1911 she put forward a young Indian, Jiddu Krishnamurti, as a World Teacher, around whom she founded the Order of the Star of India. This action seems to have provoked Steiner, who, with a large number of followers, left to found the Anthroposophical Society. The various divisions and subdivisions have continued since that time and have influenced numerous literary and intellectual figures. The groups continue to carry on active meetings.

THOTH
The Greek name for the Egyptian god of learning, wisdom and magic. In late Egyptian mythology he was the creator and orderer of the universe and the inventor of writing, arithmetic and astronomy. Thoth was depicted as an ibis-headed man carrying a pen and an ink holder or as a dog-headed baboon. In the Hellenistic period he was identified with the Greek god Hermes and in later European lore with Hermes Trismegistus, patron of magicians (*see* HERMETICA). 'The Book of Thoth' is a traditional name for TAROT cards.

THULE SOCIETY

An occult society, founded in Germany, in 1916, by Rudolf Blauer and others. Its ideas were a strange meixture of THEOSOPHISM, anti-semitism and Nordic mythology. It assumed the existence of a lost island in the far north, called Thule, which had been, like ATLANTIS, a high civilisation of superior forms of humanity that had perished in catastrophe. However, some of its teachings and craft had been preserved through the mysterious 'masters', and the unveiling of these secrets could lead to the restitution of the Nordic 'master race'. Adolf Hitler became a member of this society. Its emblem was the swastika, and this, together with much of its racist doctrines, was to become part of the trappings of the National Socialist (Nazi) movement.

TRANCE

The term is applied to a state of inwardly focused attention during which a person, although not asleep, shows little awareness of the immediate environment and exhibits a minimal response to stimuli. Throughout history, in various cultures, states of ecstatic trance have been regarded as a means of gaining spiritual visions and special powers. The body of the entranced individual is thought of as being suspended between life and death while the mind is free to explore higher realms. Sometimes the body is also trained to exhibit unusual capabilities by means of trance, as in certain yogic practices. The term 'trance' is now also applied to somewhat similar states brought on through trauma or drug use. The state induced by HYPNOSIS, however, commonly differs in some ways from that of a true trance.

TREE OF LIFE

In the KABBALAH, the Sepher Yetzira proclaims the 'ineffable Sephiroth' to be ten in number, with each of them in control of a section of the cosmos. They are envisaged as forming a cosmic Tree of Life, symbolic of the essential unity of the whole universe and of its patterns of interaction. Nine of the ten Sephiroth are set in triangles formed of two opposing and one harmonising force. On the left are the female and 'negative' forces, Binah (understanding), Geburah (power), Hod (majesty); on the left the male and 'positive' forces, Hokmah (wisdom), Hesed (love), Netsah (endurance); in the centre are the ambivalent forces, Kether (supreme crown), Tiphereth (beauty) and Yesod (foundation). Not directly linked to these triangular harmonisations is the tenth force, Malkuth (kingdom). The Tree is sometimes depicted in the form of a male human body to indicate the micro/macro aspects of the universe. Kether stands for the Prime Mover, creation. Hokmah is the active principle that drives the cosmos. Binah is the passive principle, the understanding of God. Hesed is fatherly love and authority. Geburah is severe and harsh. Tiphereth is the Sun, the life-force. Netsah is the force of nature. Hod is the force of mental power. Yesod is the sphere of the Moon, of hidden depths. Malkuth is the principle of earth and subsumes within itself the whole divine cosmos. Its number is 10, meaning all things.

TRIANGULAR LODGE

A building that is said to be the most occult building in England, at least in terms of its design and decoration. Situated at Rushton, Northamptonshire, it was built in the late sixteenth century by Sir Thomas Tresham, a Roman Catholic squire who was obsessed by NUMEROLOGY, particularly the number three, which is that of the Trinity. Thus the building is triangular in plan, with three triangular gables on each face. But there is much more numerological lore woven into the design; every number below seventy-two may be discovered by multiplication, reduction and extension. Seventy-two is a special number in the KABBALAH, a secret number.

TRIPLICITIES *see* GROUPINGS.

TWILIGHT ZONE *see* BERMUDA TRIANGLE.

U

UFO *see* FORTEAN PHENOMENA.

UNCTIONS
The name given by occultists to various annointing oils used in ceremonial magic. In WITCHCRAFT literature the word is used for the flying salve used by witches as a body oil to enable them to fly to the SABBAT. These oils were said to be produced from rotting corpses or the boiled bodies of sacrificed infants.

UNDINE
The beings associated with the ELEMENT of Water, normally represented as small creatures with fin-like wings.

VAMPIRE

In folklore, a vampire is a malign spirit that refuses to join the ranks of the dead but instead takes possession of a body in order to continue enjoying the pleasures of the living. Western notions of the vampire come primarily from Slavic folklore, especially as it was interpreted by the author Bram Stoker (1847–1912) in his novel *Dracula* (1897). In some isolated regions of eastern Europe, peasants still hang wreaths of garlic over their doors – a preventative measure cited in *Dracula* – as protection against evil spirits, but many other aspects of Stoker's story may have been his own invention.

VIRGO

The sixth sign of the ZODIAC.

dates: 24 August to 22 September.

origin and glyph: the Egyptian goddess of grain (Nidaba) was probably the origin, and in old pictures the Virgin is shown bearing an ear of corn and holding a child; the glyph is the female genitalia.

ruling planet and groupings: Mercury; feminine, mutable and earth.

typical traits: Virgoans are traditionally shy and modest, hard-working and practical and yet, perhaps, rather dull. They have a well-developed tendency to criticise both themselves and others, and often allow this to go too far. If a positive tenor is applied to Virgoan traits, it results in someone who works hard, is sensible and intelligent, and very good at detailed tasks.

Being essentially a worker, Virgoans are not interested in taking the lead but more in completing a task to the best of their ability. There is a likelihood that Virgoans will be worriers, and they often worry about nothing at all, which can be misconstrued or counterproductive. However, their own positive qualities are the best tools to deal with such problems.

family: Virgoans are very loyal in relationships and fond of their family, although this love may not manifest itself openly but rather in private. They may be self-effacing or even devalue themselves by feeling unworthy. A more common fault would be to over-criticise, but in the main they are caring, sound partners.

Children like to be kept occupied and at school will be neat, tidy and helpful. Their natural shyness may make them seem aloof, but if they can build up their self-confidence this will help them to keep worry at bay.

A great deal of time and attention will be paid to the home to keep it nice, but care should be exercised so that standards are not kept too high.

business: as already mentioned, Virgoans are not particularly ambitious and therefore are happier when supervised at work. If attention to detail is required then they are very capable and proficient in problem-solving or working in science or medicine. Although they like to be appreciated, they are happier working as a member of a team. They have an incisive style, useful in the media and the teaching profession.

wider aspects: there is a desire for purity, perfection and happiness, which, provided that their self-esteem is strong enough, is attainable through application of their own qualities.

associations: *colour* – grey, green, brown; *flowers* – bright small flowers, e.g. buttercup; *gemstone* – sardonyx (a white/brown banded variety of onyx); *trees* – nut producing varieties; *food* – root vegetables.

VOODOO

A mythico-religious system with followers predominantly in Haiti in the West Indies and in other countries to which Haitians have immigrated. Developed by African slaves brought to Haiti by the French between the seventeenth and nineteenth centuries, it combines features of African religion with the Roman Catholicism of the European settlers. Voodoo is similar in many ways to other Afro-American cults, such as Santeria in Cuba and Macumba in Brazil. The term voodoo is thought to be derived from the word for 'spirit' in the Fon language of Dahomey, now part of Nigeria. The voodoo religion involves belief in a supreme god (*le grand maitre* or *bon dieu*) and a host of spirits called *loa*. Most voodoo practices involve the *loa*, which are often identified with Catholic saints. These spirits are closely related to African gods and may represent natural phenomena – such as fire, water or wind – or dead persons, including eminent ancestors. American Indian traditions are also incorporated, including a snake cult, and there are elements of Kabbalism (see KABBALAH) and even FREEMASONRY. The spirits consist of two main groups: the *rada*, often mild and helping, and the *petro*, which may be dangerous and harmful. Voodoo rites include special ceremonies in which the *loa* have the power to make their presence known. These are characterised by music and dancing that lead the participants into a trance-like state in which they are possessed by the *loa*. The spirit temporarily displaces the astral body of the possessed person and occupies his or her physical body. The individual thus possessed is said to be mounted by the *loa* and behaves and acts as the *loa* directs, usually in a manner characteristic of the *loa* itself. Priests called *houngans* or priestesses known as *mambos* preside over these ceremonies. Like other forms of occult lore, there is a progression in voodoo from the basic initiation of a teenage child to full priesthood. But in voodoo there is no clear theory or theology; everything is ritual and practice.

Other voodoo practices include animal sacrifices and pilgrimages. The focal point of a pilgrimage is usually a Christian church identified with a particular voodoo spirit. The most important of these pilgrimages take place in July and honour Ogou (Saint James) and Ezili Danto (Our Lady of Mount Carmel). Another aspect of voodoo is called 'work of the left hand', which includes belief in ZOMBIES.

VRIL

A word coined by Sir Edward BULWER-LYTTON to represent a force of psychic vibrational energy of colossal destructive power, seen by some as a forecast of atomic energy.

W

WALPURGIS NIGHT
The eve of May Day, which also happens to be the feast day
of the German Saint Walpurgis (died 779). Long before her
time it was like HALLOWE'EN, a night on which evil spirits
were free to roam. *See also* BROCKEN.

WANDERING JEW
A character in Medieval legend who mocked Christ on the
day of the Crucifixion and as a result was condemned to roam
the world eternally.

WELLS
Wells and springs have always been invested with occult significance. The apparently inexplicable appearance of water
from the ground, and the association of water with life-giv-
ing, are among the reasons for this. Even today in Celtic countries, wells are visited for wishes to be made, and some trib-
ute to the spirit of the place is left there, usually a piece of
cloth. The 'wishing well' has the same origin.

WEREWOLF

In European folklore, a werewolf (Old English *were*, 'man') is a man who at night transforms himself or is transformed into a wolf (a process called LYCANTHROPY) and roams in search of human victims to devour. The werewolf must return to human form at daybreak by shedding his wolf's skin and hiding it. If it is found and destroyed, the werewolf dies. A werewolf who is wounded immediately reverts to his human form and can be detected by the corresponding wound on his body. Similar creatures exist in folklore worldwide: the tiger, boar, hyena, and even the cat, are 'were-animals' in areas where wolves are not found.

WHITE LADY

A ghostly spirit common to many countries, usually as an announcement of a death to come. Her origin is in the Germanic goddess Holda, who received the souls of virgin youths and maidens, and children. She is seen not only in buildings but in lonely valleys, by fords and bridges.

WHITE MAGIC *see* MAGIC.

WICCA *see* WITCHCRAFT.

WISHING WELL *see* WELLS.

WITCHCRAFT

In the modern world witchcraft is a form of nature religion, also called Wicca, that emphasises the healing arts. The term is also applied to various kinds of MAGIC practised in Asian, African and Latin American communities. What little is known about the history of witchcraft in Europe comes from hostile sources. In traditional European society witchcraft was associated with the worship of SATAN, a doctrine formulated in the late Middle Ages. Just how many of the beliefs about witches were based on reality and how many on delusion will never be known. The punishment of supposed witches by the death penalty did not become common until the fifteenth century. The first major witch-hunt occurred in Switzerland in 1427, and the first important book on the subject, the MALLEUS MALEFICARUM appeared in Germany in 1486, two years after the papal Bull *Summis Desiderantes* of 1484, which authorised death for witches.

The persecution of witches reached its height between 1580 and 1660, when witch trials became almost universal throughout western Europe. Geographically, the centre of witch-burning lay in Germany, Austria and Switzerland, but few areas were left untouched by it. No one knows the total number of victims, but informed estimates run into millions. In southwestern Germany alone, more than 3,000 witches were executed between 1560 and 1680. Not all witch trials ended in deaths. In England, where torture was prohibited, only about twenty per cent of accused witches were executed (by hanging); in Scotland, where torture was used, nearly half of all those put on trial were burned at the stake, and almost three times as many witches (1,350) were killed as in England. Some places had fewer trials than others. In the Dutch republic, no witches were executed after 1600, and none was tried after 1610. In Spain and Italy accusations of witchcraft were handled by the Inquisition, and although torture was legal, only a dozen witches were burned out of 5,000 put on trial. Ireland seems to have escaped witch trials altogether. Many witch trials were provoked not by hysterical authorities or fanatical clergy, but by village quarrels among neighbours. About eighty per cent of all accused witches were women. Traditional theology assumed that women were weaker than men and more likely to succumb to the Devil. It may in fact be true that, having few legal rights, they were more inclined to settle quarrels by resorting to magic rather than law.

All these aspects of witchcraft crossed over to the Americas with European colonists. In the Spanish and French territories cases of witchcraft were under the jurisdiction of church courts, and no one suffered death on this charge. In the English colonies about forty people were executed for witchcraft between 1650 and 1710, half of them in the famous Salem Witch Trials of 1692. Witch trials declined in most parts of Europe after 1680; in England the death penalty for witchcraft was abolished in 1736. In the late seventeenth and eighteenth centuries one last wave of witch persecution afflicted Poland and other areas of eastern Europe, but that ended by about 1740. The last legal execution of a witch occurred in Switzerland in 1782.

Beginning in the 1920s, witchcraft was revived in Europe and the United States by groups that considered it a survival of pre-Christian religious practices. Some forms of modern witchcraft follow the traditions of medieval herbalists and lay healers; the supreme law of the 'Craft' is called the Wiccan Rede: 'An [If] harm none, do what ye will'. Witches do not worship the DEVIL and blood sacrifice is forbidden. *See also* SCOT, REGINALD.

WITCHES' SABBATH *see* SABBAT.

WITCHFINDERS

During the WITCHCRAFT trials in Europe it was established legal procedure for specially appointed (or self-appointed) individuals to find or discover witches and bring them to trial. As fees were usually paid for such discoveries, the role of witchfinder was often highly lucrative. The most famous English witchfinder, the so-called Witchfinder General, was Matthew Hopkins, who in fourteen months (from 1645) had several hundred witches hanged – over a hundred at Bury St Edmunds alone. His equally notorious pricker (*see* PRICKING) was John Stearns.

WITCHMARK *see* DEVIL'S MARK.

WRAITH

The phantom, or ghostlike manifestation, of a still-living person, which is usually taken as a sign of impending death. Wraiths of persons about to die have been seen by close relatives who live far away from the source.

WYRD

From an Old Germanic word meaning fate or destiny, as in Old English *weird*, a force that is beyond human control, manipulated by divine spirits.

XYZ

XENOGLOSSY
The ability to speak in an unlearned foreign language. It is associated with past-life recall, states of trance or hypnosis and mediumship. The phenomenon is very rare. Many so-called instances turn out to be cases where the foreign language has been learned at some stage and then forgotten. When it does occur, cases where individuals recite foreign words and phrases without understanding their meaning are far more common than cases where an individual can actually *converse* intelligently in the supposedly unknown language.

YEATS, WILLIAM BUTLER (1865–1939)
This great Anglo-Irish poet was profoundly influenced by the occult, even from his boyhood days in Sligo, Ireland, among country people with stories of the SECOND SIGHT and the EVIL EYE. Later he was initiated into the ORDER OF THE GOLDEN DAWN in London. Occult symbols are frequent and fundamental in his poetry.

ZODIAC

The arc of the sky from horizon to horizon, along which the Sun travels, making 360 degrees, is divided into twelve sectors of thirty degrees each, each sector corresponding to an astrological sign and with a specific occult character and significance of its own. The word is from Greek *zodiakos*, 'pertaining to animals'. *See* ASTROLOGY; HOROSCOPE; HOUSES.

ZOMBIE

In Haitian and West African folk belief, a soulless corpse reanimated by a VOODOO priest, known as a bocor. A zombie moves listlessly in a trancelike state and does the bidding of the bocor. The term is apparently derived from Nzambi, a West African snake deity. Most cultural anthropologists working in Haiti discount stories about zombies. Some researchers, however, claim that the stories are true and that a bocor's victims are administered a powder containing a powerful neurotoxin derived from the puffer fish. The powder is alleged to paralyse the victim into a deathlike state. The bocor later revives the victim. Pharmacologists who have tested samples of the alleged powder found little or no poison in them.

ZOROASTER (*c*.628–*c*.551 BC)

A Persian philophoser who founded a religion that became the national faith of ancient Persia and is embodied in the AVESTA. A feature of this religion was a belief in a good and an evil power or deity perpetually striving against each other. The good deity is AHURA MAZDA, also known as Ormuzd, and the bad deity AHRIMAN.